Absolutely Positively
Gundog Training

Also by Robert Milner

Retriever Training for the Duck Hunter
A FEMA Disaster Search Dog-Training Model
Retriever Training—a Back-to-Basics Approach

Absolutely Positively Gundog Training

POSITIVE TRAINING FOR YOUR RETRIEVER GUNDOG

———

Robert Milner

ISBN-13: 9781514221839
ISBN: 1514221837
Library of Congress Control Number: 2015909197
CreateSpace Independent Publishing Platform
North Charleston, South Carolina

To Susan, the love of my life

Table of Contents

About the Author

———

In 1996, Robert Milner sold Wildrose Kennels, a retriever-training kennel that he had owned and operated since 1972. That same year, he retired from the US Air Force Reserve after twenty-six years of service as a disaster- response officer. Those two paths would cross in 2002. Shortly after the tragedy of 9/11, Milner got a call from the Memphis Fire Department requesting his assistance with their Federal Emergency Management Agency disaster-search dog program. He took the job and went to work rebuilding their dog program. Slow progress of the transformation led him to reexamine the traditional dog-training model of compulsion. He adopted B. F. Skinner's positive-training model and was able to speed up the training program by 300 percent. Subsequently, he adapted that training model to gundog training and discovered positive training to be much faster, easier to learn, and decidedly more fun for both dog and trainer. He has trained over two thousand dogs with compulsion and has trained hundreds of gundogs with the positive-training protocol.

CHAPTER 1
The Journey

ANYTIME A PERSON WANTS ADVICE, he should ask it from an expert who has depth of knowledge and breadth of experience in the field in question. To that end, I will recount to you my journey through the world of retriever training.

I came early to retriever field trials. I had an uncle who was a retriever field trial enthusiast and who thought that a boy of nine or ten was great for free labor to throw birds at training sessions and at retriever trials. He recruited me regularly to work at retriever field trials and occasionally for visiting professional trainers. By fifteen, I was fairly well exposed to retriever field trials and a number of the top trainers, including Jay Sweezey, Cotton Pershall, Joe Riser, Tommy Sorenson, D. L. Walters, Floyd Hayes, Billy Wunderlich, and Billy Voight. I even got a chance to meet Charlie Morgan, the dean of the early trainers. Around that time, I got a puppy and started running him in the derby stake at whatever field trials I could hitch a ride to. Needless to say, I had plenty of advice from my mentors.

After I graduated from high school, I left the dogs and went off, first to college and then a five-year tour in the Air Force.

My final Air Force assignment brought me back to the dogs. My last duty station was McChord Air Force Base at Tacoma, Washington. The two years that I was there, I lived off base and just down the road from Roy Gonia, one of the top retriever trainers in the country. I bought a six-month-old puppy from Roy and began training him. I spent a great deal of my spare time at Roy's and managed to absorb from him some dog-training knowledge.

My dog's name was Toni's Blaine Child (Canuck). He got a few places in the derby stake and, while still running the derby (under two years of age), also garnered placements in the qualifying and open stakes. Just after he turned two years of age, I sold him to a client of Tommy Sorenson. A couple of months later, Canuck got the open first place he needed to achieve the Field Champion title. Later, in the midseventies, I trained a young dog named I Like Luke of Wyntuck, who won places in the derby and open prior to turning two. Luke also achieved his Field Champion title at a young age.

In 1972, I left the active-duty Air Force while continuing in the Air Force Reserve. Upon becoming a civilian, and needing a source of income, I decided to open a dog training kennel. I started Wildrose Kennels at Grand Junction, Tennessee. I was training retrievers for gundogs and field trials. After a few years of struggling, I had developed a clientele and was running the field trial circuit. I had a big dog truck and ran the Southeast field trials in spring and fall, and the Rocky Mountain region field trials in summer.

During the seventies, my training was greatly influenced by two men who were superb horse trainers. The first was Delmar Smith. He can work magic with both horses and pointing dogs, along with a few other animals. I attended some of his seminars and absorbed as much knowledge as my youth would allow. I adopted his force-fetch model using a table and a toe hitch. I incorporated that model into my first book, *Retriever Training for the Duck Hunter*, published around 1980.

The most important thing I learned from Delmar was the study of the effectiveness of an extremely small amount of force in compulsion training. Delmar also taught me that the critical element of training an animal is, "Make it easy for the animal to do what you want."

The second influential person was Ray Hunt, the original horse whisperer. I would rate Ray Hunt among the top horse trainers in the world. I have seen him take a rank, two-year-old, fresh-off-range-in-Montana horse and, in two hours, have him saddled and walking easily under a rider. He did this without the slightest argument between horse and trainer. Ray was essentially a practitioner of positive training. He didn't use the vocabulary, but he certainly employed the principles. He never forced, but rather rewarded the behavior he wanted. To the horse, being a prey animal, space is a great reward when he is stressed. Ray was a master at granting that space in the quantity needed by each horse. Ray taught me to let the animal make the decision, while stacking the deck for the outcome you want. Ray died in 2009 and will be sorely missed by the horse world, especially the horses themselves. One of Ray's favorite sayings was, "I'm here for the horse—to help him get a better deal." I am with Ray on that thought. I feel the same about the dogs.

After I had been running field trials for eight to ten years, I had a light-bulb moment that drastically altered my course with the dogs. One spring day shortly after duck season, I was training a dog on a fairly standard field trial water blind. I was running the dog 50 yards back from the water's edge. The line to the 200-yard blind entered the water at an extremely acute angle and then continued for another 150 yards to a dead duck floating in the lake. Along the way, at about 100 yards out, the line skirted a small point passing the land at a distance of about twenty feet. I had previously dragged a duck around on the point, so that the wind would waft the duck scent out across the dog's line of travel.

I sent the dog. He sliced the angle entry perfectly and carried the line beautifully. However, when he came abreast of and down-wind of the point, he took a sharp right turn toward the duck scent filling his nose. I gave him a whistle. He didn't respond. I gave him another whistle. He didn't respond. He continued toward the point, got out on it, and started hunting. I gave him a whistle. He didn't respond. I gave him a brief shock with the electric collar. I gave him a cast toward the water. He reentered the water, and he continued on the blind retrieve, which he completed with two more whistle stops and casts.

Just about then, the light bulb popped on. I had just punished that dog in a field trial situation for the behavior I most wanted from him in a hunting situation. I had punished him for persistently hunting and following duck scent to source. That's the behavior I most want from him when I have shot a duck that has fallen crippled out 150 yards in flooded buck brush.

That was the point at which I started examining retriever field trial evaluations of dog behaviors in the light of how they related to gundogs and hunting situations. About a week later, I decided to quit training field trial dogs and concentrate on gundogs.

The next change maker in my life occurred a year or so later. I took a trip to England. One of my clients asked me to call on a friend of his, from whom he had bought a dog. When I arrived in London, I called Morty Turner-Cooke and arranged to stop by for a brief visit. The brief visit turned into an immediate move from my London hotel into Morty's home for the duration of the trip. It also turned into a long-term friendship and business relationship. Morty took me under his wing and brought me into the United Kingdom world of shooting, retrievers, and retriever trials. Morty took me shooting, arranged some retriever judging gigs, got me in line at retriever championships to take photos for magazine articles, and enabled me to meet the queen at the IGL Retriever Championship at Sandringham in 1992. Morty also arranged for me to serve a judge at the occasional retriever competition and at the *Shooting Times* Cold Game Test the year it was held at Sandringham and won by June Atkinson's great golden retriever, Holway Corbiere.

Morty Turner-Cooke died in 2013. He was a retired British Army officer who had swum off the beach at Dunkirk. He was a great sportsman, an honorable gentleman, a comrade in arms, a mentor, a valued business associate, and a treasured friend.

Through Morty, I met two United Kingdom trainers who markedly influenced my training philosophy and practice. The first was Bill Meldrum, the queen's trainer and later headkeeper at Sandringham. Bill made up seven field champions for the queen. He is a fantastic trainer and definitely a talented breeder. Bill taught me the importance of genetic behaviors in a great gundog. If the gundog is not born with the behavioral potential for greatness, then it is not going to happen through training.

The second was June Atkinson, a legend in the golden retriever community. She has produced and trained a great number of field champion goldens. She won the International Gundog League Retriever Championship in 1954 and has judged the Retriever Championship at least six times. June is another dog trainer who started with horses. She is famous in the point-to-point horse circle as a great breeder of winning horses. I met June through Morty and attended several dog-training sessions with her. I learned from her to give the dog a chance to make a mistake so that he can learn from it, and that he might have to make the mistake several times to get the lesson. My favorite memory of June is her classic answer to the question, "How do you get a dog to quit chasing pheasants?" She answered, "Let him chase them." Left unsaid was the footnote, "A smart dog will quit chasing when he finds that he cannot catch them."

On my first visit to Morty Turner-Cooke in 1982, my second light-bulb moment occurred. I went shooting and observed the manners and efficiency of the retrievers. The dogs had good manners without much attention and no noise from the handler. The dogs retrieved all the birds efficiently. The dogs sat quietly and calmly through periods of up to twenty or thirty minutes during a drive while birds were being shot all around them. The dogs quite readily, and with minimal direction, retrieved the crippled birds first.

I went to a field trial and saw the same standards. The field trial was held on a regular shoot. The tests were determined by where the bird happened to fall. The dogs were expected to be well mannered, and the handlers quiet. The valued behaviors were good manners, steadiness on driven birds, and tracking down wounded birds. These were the valued behaviors for any gundog in any country on any quarry.

The typical United Kingdom judge is unlikely to award a place to a dog who has not demonstrated sitting for driven birds and tracking down a crippled bird. You occasionally see a trial in which several awards of merit are given and no places are awarded. Most United Kingdom retriever field trial judges are very much aware of the importance to field trial titles as a driver of breeding selection and future quality of gundogs. Therefore, they take their custodianship of that quality quite seriously.

I visited trainers and got a good look at training models and quality of dog. I saw cooperative dogs and gentle-training models, with dogs and trainers enjoying their jobs. The United Kingdom trainers are fairly gentle and do not force fetch. They also do not use the electric collar. I saw trainers getting performance from their dogs with very little compulsion.

As I was flying home from that first trip, mulling over what I had seen, the light-bulb moment occurred. The United Kingdom dogs and training culture represented what retrievers should be. At that moment, I decided to change as rapidly as I could over to dogs of the United Kingdom field trial gene pool.

It took me several years, but I replaced my American breeding stock with United Kingdom breeding stock. With Morty Turner-Cooke's help, I was able to buy top-notch dogs from the United Kingdom, and I did so. The change to the British gene pool was amazing. The dogs were, in general, much more cooperative. The training became much more fun.

The change to British dogs led me inexorably into adopting more and more gentle-training methods. The British dogs are a good bit more soft and sensitive than their typical American cousins. That is a major factor in the British dogs being easier to train. I wrote a second book reflecting the more gentle training methods. *Retriever Training—a Back-to-Basics Approach* was published by DU in 2000.

By 1996, I had become quite active in the industrial real estate business and found that I didn't have the time to manage the kennel and do real estate, so I sold Wildrose Kennel to a gentleman named Ed Apple. Ed ran it a few years and then sold Wildrose to Mike Stewart in 1999.

As with many of us, my next big change came on September 11, 2001. The change began with a phone call from Tennessee Task Force One, one of the twenty-eight task forces composing the Federal Emergency Management Agency's (FEMA) National Urban Search and Rescue Response System. The typical task force is sponsored by a municipal fire department and financed by FEMA. Each task force maintains a trained, ready, and deployable body of eighty people ready to respond to structural-collapse incidents. They typically respond to presidentially declared disasters involving significant structural-collapse events. Each task force consists of rescue technicians, search technicians, medical personnel, engineers, and a complement of four search dogs with handlers. The search dogs are a vital element of the task force. A task force leader, when faced with a huge pile of rubble to search for buried victims, has to decide where to most productively deploy his meager assets to find and save the most victims. The dogs help him do that. A dog/handler team can search an acre of rubble in approximately ten to fifteen minutes. To search the same area manually would take many hours.

During the phone call, I was asked to help Tennessee Task Force One rebuild their search-dog program. The task force had deployed to the Pentagon on 9/11 and discovered that their dog program was deficient. I committed to rebuilding their dog program. I first recruited new dog handlers with a goal of 50 percent being police officers or firefighters to achieve a disaster-response culture. I then purchased young, started Labrador gundogs for the new handlers to train. The dogs lived with the handlers, and I had the handlers and dogs for a three-hour training class twice a week. At this point, I was using gentle-compulsion training.

After several months of training my handlers and dogs, I looked at the progress records and was unpleasantly surprised to see that, at our rate of progress, it was going to take eighteen months to get the team trained and certified. As a professional disaster-response officer, and from the perspective of my position as task force program manager, I found this delay unacceptable. Looking for causes brought me straight to the training model. The people were motivated and smart. The dogs were motivated and smart. I was an experienced and successful trainer of dogs and people in other areas. The compulsion-training model appeared to be the culprit.

I looked around for different animal-training models, and my military background brought me quickly to the navy's marine-mammal-training model. It was basically B. F. Skinner's operant conditioning theory as applied to marine mammals. The navy had spent a great deal of money developing the real-world applications of Skinner's theory to training dolphins to find deep-tethered underwater mines and training sea lions to retrieve objects dropped off ships in relatively shallow water.

I did a little research and found the dog form of Skinner's operant conditioning. I first learned how to do it and explored using it with our dogs and handlers. The application of Skinner's operant conditioning to dogs is popularly termed "clicker training." I was happy with the initial work and determined to convert.

I loaded our fifteen dog handlers on an airplane, and we attended a three-day Karen Pryor Clicker Training Conference at which the best trainers in the country gave classes on operant conditioning. They included dolphin trainers, dog trainers, zoo trainers, and horse trainers.

After the clicker training, we returned to Memphis and got to work implementing the positive-training program. I brought in Kathy Sdao and Steve White, two world-class clicker trainers, to give some individual coaching to our handlers. The resulting training progressed rapidly. We reduced the initial projected eighteen months for compulsion training to six months for positive training. That was a 300 percent reduction in learning curve for novice trainers. That told me that positive training is three times easier for a novice trainer to master.

I worked for the task force for three years as the task force manager and deployed several times with them in various capacities including dog handler, search team manager, and task force leader.

In 2005, I left the task force and started Duckhill Kennels to breed better Labradors for gundogs, disaster-search dogs, and explosive-detection dogs. I started experimenting with positive training for those three functions and developed the practical models to apply to produce the behaviors needed.

The gundog-training model turned out to be extremely simple. It took me a while to get enough outside of my box to develop the applications, but I succeeded. Now, by 2015, I have proofed the positive gundog-training model on over two hundred gundogs, and it works very well.

CHAPTER 2

The Dog

———

IF YOU WANT TO DO a good job as a dog trainer, you need to have some knowledge of your subject, the dog. What does he see? What does he hear? What does he smell? How does he learn? Most important is; how does he communicate? A little information on these topics will make your job much easier and will take your training project to higher degrees of excellence.

HIS ORIGINS AND EVOLUTION

DNA studies have shown that all dogs have evolved from the Eurasian gray wolf. The first archaeological evidence of domestic dogs indicates the earliest domestication at approximately fourteen thousand years ago. Since that time, the dog has proven himself to be a skilled and talented adapter to the company of humans. In contrast to most other mammals, the dog has continued to increase in numbers and geographic expansion.

During the early portion of the dog's domestication, man was basically a hunter/gatherer with an uncertain and unpredictable food supply. The dog's earliest value to man probably lay in guarding, hunting, and herding, three behaviors natural to the dog. The dog probably also had great early value as an emergency food supply. That would have ruthlessly driven a selection process favoring the most valuable dogs in terms of function, intelligence, and communication skills. Dogs evolved to excel at reading and anticipating what people wanted or intended to do. They became masters at reading a person's body language, eye movements, and intentions. Those that did not ended up roasting over the village fire in times of food shortage. The dogs that had the most value were the dogs that survived the longest. With an evolutionary history like this, a dog is not capable of willful disobedience, a characteristic that many trainers seem prone to attach to the dog.

His Basic Nature

The world of dogs is poorly understood and greatly distorted by myth and folklore. It is also distorted by a lack of research and valid information. Until recently, the dog has been virtually neglected by the animal behavior research community. There has been more dog behavioral research conducted in the past ten years than was conducted in the previous one hundred years. A number of myths have been dispelled.

A major myth is the importance of dominance in a dog's life and social structure. The traditional picture we have had of dominance in dogs was derived from observations of wolves in contrived, artificial packs in very large pens. The advent of modern radio tracking devices has allowed detailed studies of wolf behavior in their natural environment. We have found that the typical wolf pack is eight to ten wolves consisting of a dominant breeding pair and prior years' offspring. It operates as a cooperative family group. The old dominance-and-subordinance model is a highly questionable concept in light of today's knowledge.

Some groundbreaking research that challenges traditional dog lore has been conducted by Brian Hare of Duke University. Dr. Hare's research has upended a number of traditional views of dogs.

Here are some excerpts from *The Genius of Dogs* by Brian Hare and Venessa Woods (Plume Books, 2013).

In wolves, with the exception of very large packs, a single breeding pair is dominant to everyone else. This pair uses their dominance to suppress the breeding of other pack members. Dominant female wolves are aggressive all year round and use unprovoked attacks to prevent other females from mating.

Younger and subordinate pack members are usually the offspring of the breeding pair from previous years.

To earn their keep, juveniles help their parents raise the next generation. Juveniles bring back food to pups after a successful hunt and protect the pups while their parents are hunting.

Feral dogs have a different system. While some feral dog groups have a dominance hierarchy that predicts priority of access to resources such as food and mating partners, this hierarchy is not as strict as in wolves. There is no dominant pair that leads the group. Instead, the leader of a feral pack is the dog who has the most friends. When the pack decides where to go, they do not follow the most dominant dog; instead, they follow the dog with the strongest social network.

It appears that the traditional view of dominance and subordinance has limited bearing on dog training.

THE DOG'S INTELLIGENCE

The very small amount of research that we currently have suggests that dogs are very smart in a comparison with other mammals, including primates. Here is what Brian Hare and Venessa Woods have to say in *The Genius of Dogs*:

Dog's cognitive ability relative to other animals
(Relative to other animals, dogs are):

Genius
- -Comprehending visual gestures
- -Learning new words

Remarkable
- -"Talking" through vocalizations and visual signals
- -Understanding an audience's perspective
- -Copying others' actions
- -Recruiting Help

Here is what Hare and Woods say about comprehending visual gestures:

Wolves might be better than dogs at trial-and-error learning, but no one would argue that wolves are easier to train than dogs.

A dog will always learn from a human faster than a wolf, because dogs have evolved skills to read our communicative signals. While working dogs might be more skilled at using human gestures as a result of either training or human selection for this skill, all dogs are skilled at using human gestures. Even shelter dogs and breeds not intentionally bred by humans are skilled at using human gestures.

If working breeds were selected for their cooperative and communicative abilities, they should be better at following human gestures than nonworking breeds. Victoria Webber and I chose huskies and shepherds as our working breeds, since both respond to verbal and hand signals when transporting humans or herding animals. As our nonworking breeds, our control case, we chose basenjis. From my introduction to them in Congo, I know that while basenjis help their owners hunt, they are more like sight hounds—they simply chase and corner their prey and do not rely on human signals to hunt (similar to hunting behavior observed in the dogs of the Mayangna people of Nicaragua). As our other nonworking breed, we chose toy poodles, since they were largely bred based on their appearance.

The results were that while all four breeds were skilled at using human gestures, huskies and shepherds were more so than basenjis and toy poodles. Working dogs were three times more successful than nonworking dogs at using multiple types of human gestures to find hidden food. It seems that while all breeds (including New Guinea Singing Dogs and dingoes) can use human social gestures, working dogs are the most skilled of all.

It was suspected that dogs are more socially skilled than primates and wolves because they (dogs) are heavily exposed to people throughout their lifetime. In a surprise finding, young puppies with little exposure to humans are as skilled at using human gestures as adult dogs are.

This research says that dogs are extremely attuned to learning from people and that dogs have an innate talent on the scale of genius with respect to responding to directional cues from people. That tells me that our traditional retriever-training models are ten times more complicated and ten times more lengthy than they need to be. Many traditional training models actually interfere with learning in a smart dog.

THE DOG'S EARS

A dog's ears are approximately four times more sensitive than a human's ears. Thus, the sound a human can hear at twenty-five yards, a dog can hear at one hundred yards. The sensitivity of the dog's hearing has two powerful impacts upon his training and upon his gundog job. Number one is the relative ease with which his ears can be damaged by too much noise. If his ears are four times more sensitive than yours, then they are four times more susceptible to damage from the loud noise of a shot. When you are shooting, be careful of the location of his head relative to the muzzle blast of your shotgun. Be very careful in metal-pit blinds. If you keep your dog down in the bottom of the pit while shooting, he will go deaf quickly. Try remaining seated in the pit while the other occupants are shooting, and you will understand the intensity of the noise levels. Multiply that volume by four for a dog's ears.

Another factor to consider is the volume of your whistle. If you train the dog to respond to a high-volume whistle blast when he is close to you, then when he is two hundred yards away, he is not going to get the volume of whistle for which he has been trained. When you read the section on cue discrimination, you will learn that during initial training and during all work within thirty to forty yards, the whistle volume should be quite low. I frequently use a simple, forceful "hiss" noise produced by forcing air over my tongue instead of a whistle when the dog is inside thirty to forty yards. A "hiss" is also very handy when you are fumbling around, looking for your whistle.

A further pertinent factor is how the dog uses his ears to locate a downed bird. All dogs have inherited from their wolf ancestors a propensity to use their ears to locate prey. A good account of this behavior is given in Canadian author Farley Mowatt's 1963 book, *Never Cry Wolf*, a story of Mowatt's summer spent observing a small pack of arctic wolves near the Arctic Circle. Mowatt found that most of the wolves' summer diet consisted of mice, and that the wolf has a very stylized, inherited behavior for mouse hunting.

When a wolf hunts mice, he simply does a few stiff-legged bounces in the brush to stir up the prey. Then he stops and listens. When he hears a rustle, he focuses on it with a few minor head-and-ear movements. Then he crouches and pounces on the mouse, pinning it with his forepaws, before snapping it up in his mouth. All of this activity is accomplished without ever seeing the mouse. Some research has shown that the wolf can echolocate a mouse rustling in the brush six feet away and pounce and pin it with his forepaws within a half centimeter of error.

This hardwired ancestral behavior is also used to echolocate a downed duck by its splash or by its thump on hitting the ground. Your dog does not necessarily need to see a fall in order to get a good "fix" on its location. This ability especially applies at night.

THE DOG'S NOSE

The dog's nose is truly a wonder far beyond human comprehension. In 2002, Sandia National Laboratories conducted a study on nose sensitivity of trained explosive-detection dogs and determined that an explosive-detection dog could detect a target odor down in the range of one hundred parts per trillion. They had to determine the concentration by dilution and extrapolation, as we don't have instruments that will measure that extreme level of dilution. In the words of Sandia Laboratories, that concentration is the "equivalent to one molecule per sniff."

Much of a dog's brain is devoted to odor processing. Because a dog depends heavily on scent information to interpret his world, scent heavily influences his behavior. Most of the odors that are influencing him are undetectable to scent-challenged humans. Whenever the dog fails to operate as you wish, remember the power of odor as a distraction to a dog.

Remember that a human is not equipped to tell a dog where or when to detect an odor or how to react to it. Only the dog knows.

THE DOG'S EYES

Dogs are looking at you much more than you think. They have a visual field of 250 degrees compared to the human field of 190 degrees. By human standards, this extra peripheral vision allows the dog to see a lot more than we are aware of.

The two types of vision receptor cells are rods and cones. Rods detect light and dark, while cones detect color. Humans have a higher percentage of cones than dogs, with the lower cone ratio giving the dog an estimated six-times-poorer eye for detail compared to humans. On the other hand, dogs have many more rods than humans and can consequently see in light at a five-times-lower level than humans.

A higher percentage of rods allows the dog to detect motion much better than humans. This superior motion-detection capability gives dogs a wide range of communication skills. In observing other animals and people, dogs read posture and other behavior nuances with great adeptness.

Dogs have relatively poor color vision. They have only two kinds of color receptors compared to the three kinds possessed by humans. The dog's color vision is similar to that of a human with red-green color blindness.

THE DOG'S COMMUNICATION

To the trainer, communicating with the dog is the most important aspect of dog training. To train the dog, you have to be able to communicate what you want the dog to do. The trainer who knows how the dog communicates will be a much more successful trainer.

The dog communicates with sound for two basic scenarios: advertising his territory and circumventing a fight. The wolf advertises his territory by howling. The dog advertises his territory by barking. The dog's territory might consist of his yard or his owner's house or his owner's car.

The wolf growls to avoid a fight. The growl is an attempt to establish dominance without a fight, as fighting has a negative survival value in evolutionary terms. The dog practices the same behavior of attempting to communicate dominance with a growl.

Beyond those two audible scenarios, and a small degree of territorial communication with odors and noses, virtually all the dog's communication is with his eyes. When a person takes a pack of ten or fifteen dogs for an hour of hiking, a whole lot of communication will occur among the dogs, but no audible sound will be heard beyond the rustling of leaves and grass. Dogs communicate vast amounts of information to each other through body posture, motion, attitude, and movement. They communicate nearly nothing with sound.

Research has shown that dogs are quite good at reading eye movements to determine a person's intended behavior. One can infer that they do the same with other dogs.

There are two lessons for the trainer on communication. One is to be quiet when you are training a dog. Noise simply creates distraction and interferes with the training process.

The second lesson is that the trainer needs to move a little to furnish the dog with information. The trainer who stands stiffly and is immobile does not give the dog much information to read, causing the dog to become uneasy. The dog is more comfortable when there is at least a little movement coming from the trainer. This motion allows the dog to better read your intent. For those trainers who tend to stand stiffly, a good practice is to subtly walk in place as you train. This movement allows you to better communicate with the dog.

CHAPTER 3

Pick a Dog That Fits

———

A FRIEND OF MINE ONCE told me, "If you want to train a good duck-dog, then start with a good dog." He was right. I would add to that, "Start with a good dog that fits you." The retriever that fits most duck hunters is smart, easy to train, and pleasant to have around the house, and gets all the ducks.

The duck hunter needs a smart, easy-to-train dog, because most are not looking for a second job as a dog trainer. The duck hunter needs a pleasant-to-have-around dog, because most of the dog's time is spent being a companion and a family dog. Additionally, he needs a dog that sits quietly in the blind when the birds are working and the guns are shooting.

All retrievers don't possess the attributes of a great gundog. They come in a great variety of personality types. Important differences are those concerning drive and game-finding initiative, demeanor and personality, intelligence and trainability, and natural delivery to hand. As I describe these traits, I will tell you how to measure and evaluate a dog relative to these attributes. The measurement exercises are valid for dogs that are nine months and older and at least "partially trained" with the exception of the delivery-to-hand trait. Here are some ways of looking at a started or trained dog or the parents of a litter you are considering.

DRIVE AND GAME-FINDING INITIATIVE

We tend to think that more drive is better. That is wrong. Over the past twenty or thirty years, we have gradually been selectively breeding more and more drive in field retrievers. Today, we are breeding a fair number of dogs with too much drive for a novice trainer and handler to deal with. I consider a trainer a novice until he has trained thirty to forty dogs; therefore, most duck hunters fall in the novice trainer category. An overdriven dog does not "fit" the typical duck hunter.

I look at drive as having a visual reactivity component and a hunting persistence component. Some dogs are overreactive to falling objects. The sight of a falling bird or the arc of a thrown dummy elicits a strong biochemical reaction in that dog's brain that makes it extremely difficult for him to learn self-control, steadiness, and calmness in a hunting environment. An overreactive dog tends to run in front of his brain and his nose. He has trouble learning to dig cripples out of heavy cover. A good test for an overreactive dog is to find a woven-wire fence with a gate in it. With the gate open, move thirty or forty feet back from the fence and thirty feet to the left or right of the open gate. Throw a light-colored dummy across the fence to where the dog can see it lying on the ground. Send him for it. If he adjusts his course en route and goes through the gate to get to the dummy, he is great gundog material. If he runs to the fence and paws at it a little, hunts for another route, and goes through the gate, he is good. If he runs into the fence and does not find the gate but stays at the same place trying to get at the dummy or bird, he is a poor candidate.

Game-finding initiative is the most important component of drive. You might also call it "hunt drive." The test is fairly easy. Toss a bird into heavy cover and see how long the dog keeps hunting for it. Even better is tossing a clipped-wing pheasant into cover and seeing if the dog can track it down. Hunting persistence is the behavior you are looking for. The longer he persists in hunting, the better he is.

DEMEANOR AND PERSONALITY

Some dogs are too aloof and desire little interaction with people. Some dogs are too needy. Some dogs are so laid-back that they aren't particularly interested in retrieving. Some dogs are so "wired" that they seldom can relax. None of these extremes are desirable.

1. Calmness: With the dog sitting (either on or off leash), throw five or six training dummies to land within thirty to forty feet of the dog. Then move around slightly and slowly at the periphery of his visual field. How long does it take for him to relax and shift some attention to you? The faster it is, the more likely he is to tend toward calmness in the family setting.
2. "Connection with people": Take the dog for a walk off leash. Notice how close he stays to you and how often he "checks in" or looks at you. If he generally stays in sight and checks in, or returns to you, or looks at you fairly frequently, he is "connected to people" fairly well. These traits make a good gundog candidate. If he is seldom in sight and generally oblivious to you, he is a poor candidate.

INTELLIGENCE AND TRAINABILITY

Intelligence and trainability are closely related and very important. It is much more pleasant to live and hunt with a smart, cooperative dog. I measure the traits to a great degree by asking these two questions: "How long did it take to train the dog?" and "What was the skill level of the trainer?" If the dog required three or four months to train, and the trainer was a typical duck hunter who has trained two or three dogs, then that dog and his puppies have an extremely high probability of being a great fit for a duck hunter.

If the dog required ten or twelve months of training from a professional trainer and required a lot of force in the training program, then that dog and his puppies are probably a very poor fit for the duck hunter.

If you are looking at a started or trained dog or at the sire or dam of a litter, ask the dog owner to tell you about the dog's training history. That information should tell you a lot.

NATURAL DELIVERY TO HAND

The Labrador retriever has been selectively bred for gentle delivery to hand for the past two hundred years. It is a genetically inherited behavior. If you are looking at a dog either to buy or as the parent of a puppy to purchase, you want the dog who possesses this inherited behavior. Ask whether the dog naturally delivered to hand as a puppy. Ask if he had to be force-fetch trained. If he had to be force-fetch trained to achieve delivery to hand, then he is not a good fit for the duck hunter. Force-fetch training can take up to three months and takes training skills that most duck hunters don't possess.

A good duckdog is a pleasure to have. With luck, you will have his companionship for ten years or more. It pays handsomely to exercise care in the selection process. If you do, then you will have a companion that greatly enhances your outdoor experiences and serves as a treasured family member.

CHAPTER 4

Training the Gundog

———

HUNTERS HAVE BEEN TRAINING SPORTING dogs the same way for the past several hundred years. Our traditional training model has been to make the dog perform a behavior and associate a command with that behavior. We traditionally have made the dog perform with choke collars, pinch collars, and, lately, electric collars.

Today there is a much better way to train dogs. It is called operant conditioning with positive reinforcement. This training model has arisen over the past thirty to forty years. With positive training, you reward the behaviors you want and ignore the behaviors you don't want. That removes most punishment from the training program. It also makes the training much more fun for both the dog and the trainer.

Operant conditioning as an animal-training model arose during the fifties and sixties, with origins in the work of B. F. Skinner and Konrad Lorenz.

B. F. Skinner was the Edgar Pierce Professor of Psychology at Harvard University from 1958 until his retirement in 1974. He established a model of learning termed "operant conditioning."

Konrad Lorenz was an Austrian zoologist, ethologist, and ornithologist. He shared the 1973 Nobel Prize in Physiology or Medicine with Nikolaas Tinbergen and Karl von Frisch. Lorenz studied instinctive behavior in animals. Prior to Lorenz, we had looked at animal behavior as being the behaviors performed by animals in zoo cages. Lorenz brought the perspective of studying animal behavior in the animal's natural environment. Knowledge of a dog's instinctive behavior is extremely important for a dog trainer to know, since these instinctive behaviors are the basis of the trainer's work. These instinctive behaviors are also the source of significant levels of distraction that interfere with training.

Initially, the applications of Skinner's operant conditioning with positive reinforcement in animal settings were made by dolphin trainers. The US Navy spent a good bit of money in the sixties and seventies developing training protocols for dolphins, sea lions, and other marine mammals. The dolphins were trained to locate tethered mines hundreds of feet below the ocean's surface where the cold, darkness, and water pressure are far too great for humans to survive. Dolphins, with their innate sonar system that works well in these extreme conditions, are ideal candidates for this demanding and dangerous job.

The dolphin must perform this job far out of sight of his handler and while swimming through schools of fish. These fish are not only his natural food, but also constitute the rewards used in training. The trained dolphin serves as an eloquent example of the effectiveness of operant conditioning with positive reinforcement and the reliability of this training model for extremely difficult behaviors in extremely difficult environments.

Today, operant conditioning with positive reinforcement is the animal-training model used by all major zoos worldwide. Zoos require an effective animal-training model. Zoo personnel must move large, dangerous animals from one location to another and perform medical procedures on these animals. One great example is the elephant. Elephants need their toenails trimmed frequently. This task is done by training the elephant to stick his foot through the bars, rest it on a block, and let his toenails be trimmed. Also, elephants need periodic blood samples to test for tuberculosis. To enable this procedure, an elephant is trained with positive reinforcement to kneel, put its head up against the bars of its enclosure, and allow a keeper to draw blood from a vein behind the ear. The fast and widespread adoption of operant conditioning by most zoos supports the training model's effectiveness and utility.

Modern horse training has also favored a large swing to positive-training techniques. The horse, being a prey animal, has a different set of rewards than does a predator like the dog. Rewards for a horse include "space" or having an escape route, treats, and gentle stroking. Horse trainers using operant conditioning will typically use a round pen to enable giving the horse "space" in a controlled manner. The rapid and widespread adoption of the "horse whisperer" model of operant conditioning is testimony to the model's effectiveness.

OPERANT CONDITIONING

With his system of operant conditioning, B. F. Skinner transformed animal training from an art with a significant apprenticeship requirement to a craft with the characteristics of a technology. Operant conditioning is:

1. Repeatable and general. It works on animals, people, fish, etc.
2. Easy to learn. My experience with fifteen novice dog handlers shortly after 9/11 demonstrated to me conclusively that the positive-training model is three times easier to learn than the traditional compulsion-training model.

   Guide Dogs for the Blind has approximately sixty-five trainers turning out about three hundred trained guide dogs yearly. They produce a highly trained dog that holds down a complex job and that requires a certain degree of care and continuation training from the human side of the team. In 2005, Guide Dogs for the Blind changed their training model from the traditional compulsion method to positive training. After the transition, they experienced a huge increase in the pass rate of the dogs graduating from the training program. They also experienced a huge reduction in the time required for the sight-impaired handlers to master the continuing-training model needed to keep the dogs sharp.

3. Fast results. Operant conditioning with positive reinforcement can produce remarkably fast results with the trainee. My favorite example is my wife. She loves to see wild turkeys, of which we have quite a few. One day, she was driving across the bridge over a creek near our farm. She looked downstream at a sandbar and saw six wild turkeys. She became quite excited. This sighting constituted a major reward. The cue was driving across the bridge. The behavior was looking downstream at the sandbar. This occurred in 2010. As of today, 2015, the behavior remains fluent. Every time my wife drives across the bridge, she looks downstream at the sandbar. This practice is a result of a one-time trial of learning a behavior that currently has a persistence of four years and going. A well-timed reward can produce fantastic and fast results.

Operant conditioning boils down to five rules.

1. A behavior that is followed by a reward tends to be repeated.
2. A reward creates an attraction for the specific location where it was received (including proximity of trainer).
3. A behavior that is not followed by a reward tends to become extinct.
4. A behavior that is followed by a punishment tends to not be repeated.
5. A punishment creates an avoidance of the specific location in which it was received (including an avoidance of proximity to trainer).

Positive training predominantly uses rule 1, rewarding the behavior you want.

As with most other endeavors in life, you will need a little more knowledge than just the five rules given above. You will need some knowledge of the principles and how to apply them. Over the past ten years, I have used positive training and have worked out models, behavior sequences, and protocols that work quite well to train a gundog. Along with these models and sequences, you will need some understanding of the basic factors of positive training. The most important of these factors are reward and distraction.

REWARDS: COOKIE OR RETRIEVE? COKE MACHINE OR SLOT MACHINE?

Technically a reward is a reinforcer, which, when it follows a behavior, increases the probability of that behavior recurring. Practically speaking, a reward is something that the dog wants. It can be an edible treat. A reward can also be the opportunity to perform a behavior, especially a strong, instinctive behavior such as hunting, chasing, or retrieving. A reward can also be another trained behavior that has high value as a result of numerous reinforcements with a high-value reinforcer.

Many training failures are due to the trainer's faulty perception of reward. The dog is the only valid judge of what is a reward. The trainers with the most success with positive training are those who recognize what the particular dog's high-value rewards are and who are adept at delivering one of those rewards at the time the dog needs reinforcement.

Some rewards are also major distractors. A retrieve of a fallen object is a very high-value reward. The fall of a retrievable object is also a very high-level distraction. In a positive gundog-training program, we use a retrieve as a reward for the dog sitting calmly while retrievable objects fall. We put the retrieve reward nearly immediately on a variable schedule of reinforcement because of its extremely high distraction level.

Remember that the dog is the only judge of what constitutes a reward. The trainer's opinion is irrelevant. If you think the dog should work hard to get a piece of plain-old dog food or petting and praise, you might be in for a surprise. The value of a reward is reflected in how much the dog wants it and, consequently, how hard he will work to get it.

One of the most important characteristics of a reward in training a dog is that the reward be with you when the behavior occurs, so that you can deliver the reward in a timely manner (within two seconds). If delivery of reward is delayed, the dog tends to correlate the reward with whatever behavior happens to be occurring just prior to delivery of the reward.

REWARDS AND RELATIVE VALUES

Treats: With growing puppies, food treats usually trump all other rewards. Treats that typically have high value to a dog are small cheese cubes, hot dog slices, and small chunks of freeze-dried beef liver. I like the freeze-dried liver chunks because they are fairly neat and clean, and thus are more likely to be in my pocket when I need one.

A primary condition for a food reward to be of high value is that the dog be hungry. Some dogs do a lot better if a few hours have elapsed since feeding time. A special case is retriever puppies. They grow at such a rapid rate for the first six months of life that most of them are voraciously hungry all the time. This makes many retriever puppies pick a food treat over a retrieve reward, especially if it's been a few hours since a meal. As the puppy's growth rate slows after six months, the retrieve reward will begin to surpass the food treat in the ranking of value.

Tug: Tug is an expression of the dog's prey drive. Tug is a very useful reward, particularly for retrievers. It is a reward that is always handy. Young puppies have a strong propensity to play tug. Occasionally you may encounter a puppy with a suppressed tug tendency. For reluctant tuggers, tie a six-foot string to a soft, fluffy toy or piece of towel and pull it around a bit to tease the puppy. Let him catch it and pull on it. Initially, let the puppy win by allowing the puppy to get the toy after a brief tug or two. Gradually lengthen the duration of the tug game while keeping the puppy successful.

There is a very pervasive myth that tug with retrievers will make them hard of mouth. That is false. One merely trains the puppy to release on cue. It takes two to play tug. When you want the tug to cease, let go of your end. Hold the dog by his collar with one hand, have him sit, and offer him a treat with the other. You have the dog sit so that he can no longer back away; thus, he can't tug. Put the release on cue.

Retrieve: With several hundred years of selective breeding to nurture a strong retrieving instinct, retrieving is obviously a high-value reward for retrievers.

Hunting: The act of hunting is also a reward. Knowing this enables you to counteract it. An example would be whistle stopping. If you send the pup out 150 yards and give him a stop whistle, and he continues hunting, the hunting is a payment. Give him a couple more whistles. If he responds, pull your dummy launcher out and shoot a long, high dummy out to him as a payment for stopping. The payment retrieve has much more value than the act of hunting. Rerun the blind, and you probably won't get whistle refusals. Rerunning the blind will produce a behavior chain of:

Go out...stop...cast...stop...cast...stop...cast...reward (find dummy).

Petting and praise: Petting and praise are both relatively low-value rewards for most dogs. If you want a demonstration, have someone give him a small piece of cheese. Then start petting him while the cheese person steps away and drops another small piece of cheese on the floor. It the dog leaves the petting to get the cheese, the answer is fairly obvious.

Another issue with petting and praise is that we humans deliver it all the time regardless of whether the dog is in a training situation or not. The high frequency with which we deliver petting and praise dilutes its value. If you want to get the highest value for petting and praise as a training tool, then you should only bestow it in a training scenario.

Whatever the dog wants: Anything the dog wants can be used as a reward. If the dog likes to chase squirrels and needs improvement at heeling, you can use the opportunity to chase a squirrel as a reward for heeling a certain distance. Then, gradually increase the distance required for the pup to "buy" the reward of chasing a squirrel. A flexible and imaginative trainer who pays attention to his dog's interactions with his environment can find many different rewards to use in training the dog.

Other rewards: Attention is a reward to a dog and comes in many forms. Simply looking at a dog can be rewarding to the dog. If you look at the case of a dog jumping up and putting paws up on a person, the person typically looks at the dog, pushes on the dog, and makes noise. All of these behaviors are rewards to the dog. That is why some people have a lot of trouble getting the dog to stop jumping up on them. If you want to remove the rewards, simply fold your arms on your chest and turn 180 degrees from the dog. This action will remove all the rewards.

The quickest, easiest way to stop a dog that jumps up on people is to reward sitting sufficiently so that the dog's automatic behavior upon approaching a person is to sit.

In dog training, the better your grasp of reward value is, the better will be your training.

TIMING

A major characteristic of an effective reward is that it be delivered immediately after the performance of a desired behavior. If it is a food reward, it needs to be in your pocket and quickly accessible. If you have to walk thirty feet to get the treat in order to deliver it, then you will be rewarding all the behaviors that occurred during the time it took you to walk over and get the treat.

Similarly, if you find yourself needing to deliver a retrieve reward for a whistle stop and don't have a dummy handy, by the time you get the dummy and throw it, the dog will have been through several other behaviors before you can deliver the reward.

Whatever behavior was occurring just prior to the delivery of the reward is the behavior that is most reinforced by delivery of the reward.

MARKERS

Sometimes you need to "mark" or identify a behavior in a situation where you can't deliver the reward quickly enough. The dog might be too far away for you to immediately deliver a reward. In this case, you need a "marker." I use a clicker. A clicker is a small, plastic box with a piece of metal that you press with your thumb to produce a distinct "click." The click is used as an audible marker to mark a specific behavior or piece of behavior. You might think in terms of a camera. The click says to the dog, "Yes! That is the exact behavior I want." The clicker also acts as an IOU. It says to the dog, "I am going to pay you in the next few seconds." After a number of repetitions of the click being followed by a reward, the clicker becomes rewarding in itself. It is called a secondary reinforcer. As long as you keep following the click with a primary reinforcer, such as a treat or a retrieve, the click will retain its value as a secondary reinforcer.

Many people like to use a verbal marker such as "good dog." That is not as good a marker. To initiate the verbal marker takes a split second longer, as the thought has to go to the brain's speech center and then to the larynx. The other drawback of a verbal marker is the duration of the marker. During the time I initiate and then finish the phrase "good dog," the dog has been through several more behaviors. It is difficult for him to know which behavior I am talking about. The click is an immensely more valuable marker than the voice because the click is extremely fast to initiate and is extremely brief in duration. The click much more precisely defines a particular behavior.

Schedules of Reinforcement and Persistence of Behavior

There are basically two schedules of reinforcement you need to know about.

The first is a constant schedule of reinforcement in which you reward every repetition of the behavior. The constant schedule is used in initially building a behavior and in shaping and distraction-proofing that behavior. After the behavior is fluent in the face of distraction, it should be put on a variable schedule of reinforcement to develop persistence of the behavior.

A constant schedule of reinforcement can be compared to a Coke machine. If I go up to a Coke machine one hundred times and perform the behavior of inserting a dollar and pushing a button, I will be rewarded on a constant schedule of reinforcement. The behavior is putting the dollar in and pushing the Coke button. The reward is the Coke.

If I go up to the Coke machine the 101st time, perform the behavior, and do not receive a Coke, I will be taken aback. I will probably try one more time. If on the 102nd repetition I insert the dollar, push the button, and receive again nothing, I will probably quit. The behavior is extinct. The behavior has very low persistence.

Look, on the other hand, at a slot machine. If I go up to a slot machine and perform one hundred times the behavior of inserting a dollar and pulling the handle, I will be paid on a random, unpredictable schedule. If on the 101st repetition I receive no reward, I will still pull the handle. I will probably keep pulling the handle in spite of no payment for a very large number of times. Some people can never quit.

The slot machine is a variable schedule of reinforcement. It is unpredictable. It makes a behavior highly persistent. That is the schedule upon which you need to put your dog's rewards for a behavior in order to make the behavior resistant to extinction. Then you don't have to take treats to the duck blind with you.

Understanding and smart use of rewards, including use of variable schedules of reinforcement, are key elements to making training effective.

Rewards are also cumulative in in value. A number of small rewards add up to a large value. A clear example of this would be training a puppy with a food reward to maintain his sit on a place board, while increasing distraction over a number of sessions until he can sit on the place board while a tennis ball is bounced in front of him. Several sessions with a number of treat rewards for sitting on the board will outweigh the extremely high distraction value of a bouncing tennis ball. See Chapter 10 for a full discussion of place board training.

DISTRACTION: EXCUSE FOR MISBEHAVIOR OR TRAINING TOOL?

A very common comment is, "My dog works great in the yard, but when I take him hunting, he acts like he has never learned anything." That is a classic case of going from the yard with no distraction to the hunting scenario, which is a superhigh-distraction environment, with no intermediate steps.

An understanding of distraction is essential to a trainer of animals or of people. Distraction is the amount and intensity of other stimuli in the environment. For a dog to be proficient in a behavior, he must be able to perform that behavior well in the presence of distractions.

A dog is a poor generalizer. He can learn a behavior in a plain and simple environment fairly easily. A prime example is a dog that performs whistle stops and hand signals faultlessly in the backyard. If you then take that dog from the backyard straight to the actual hunting situation, he will probably perform poorly. The leap from low distraction to multiple, high distractions is too abrupt and too high.

A good human example of training for distraction would be training a young person in public speaking.

If you take a fifteen-year-old human and teach him to perform the behavior of public speaking in his living room, speaking to his family of five people, he will gain proficiency quite rapidly. You can get him perfect in that living room with those five people. If you then put him in an auditorium in front of people, he will probably fail at public speaking. The failure is attributable to making a too high a jump in distraction level. The appropriate training program would have been to first gradually increase the number of people in the living room. First, have him speak to 20 or 30 people in a small auditorium, then 100 in the same small auditorium, then 50 in a large auditorium, then 150 in a large auditorium, then 300 in a large auditorium, and finally 500 in the large auditorium. With the gradual training program in the face of gradually increasing distraction level, you will have vastly increased the speaker's probability of success.

I encountered a graphic lesson in distraction training when I took a load of dogs to Montana last summer. The day after I arrived, I set up a routine training scenario in a cow pasture and neglected to account for the distraction levels. The first three dogs acted like idiots. I ceased the training and restructured.

The week before, in Tennessee, I was training in high humidity, high temperature, three hundred feet of altitude, short grass, no cattle, and no strange game animals.

In Montana, I was training in low humidity, cool temperature, six thousand feet of altitude, twenty-four-inch grass, cattle and cattle manure, elk scent and manure, and mule deer scent and manure. I had set up a training scenario, expecting performance levels the same as the week before in Tennessee. That was a mistake.

I reset the training scenario from a 150-yard blind retrieve to a 30-yard blind retrieve and removed the diversion marks. Then the dogs were able to perform decently. Over the next couple of days, I gradually extended the distances to 150 yards and added back the diversion marks.

Some typical and common distractions for retrievers can be categorized as follows:

1. **Odor**: A dog has a phenomenally sensitive sense of smell. Sandia Laboratories did a study in 2002 with trained explosive-detection dogs to determine how low a concentration of a target odor a dog can detect. Sandia found that a trained explosive-detection dog can detect a target odor down in the range of one hundred parts per trillion. They had determined the concentration by dilution and extrapolation, because we don't have instruments capable of measuring concentrations that dilute. In Sandia's words, the dog's sensitivity to a target odor is approximately "one molecule per sniff." That is an odor level that we cannot measure and that we have great difficulty even conceptualizing. Many times you will find yourself wondering why a dog is not succeeding at a task. Frequently, the culprit will be an odor that is extremely distracting to the dog, but not detectable by a human. The dog has a sensitivity to odor that a human cannot even begin to appreciate.

2. **Sound**: New, strange sounds or conditioned sounds such as gunshots are distractions.

The category of sound distractions includes your voice. When you are initially training and shaping a behavior, keep your mouth shut. Your voice simply serves as a distraction and makes it harder for the dog to learn. Wait until the behavior is fluent in low distraction before you start talking. Then your voice will be one of the many distractions that you add in later to increase the fluency of the behavior in increasing distraction levels.

3. **Sights**: New, visible objects, people, or other animals are also distractions. Moving animals and objects tend to be highly distracting.
4. **Cover**: Cover tends to stimulate the dog's hunting instinct; plus, it holds lots of odors.
5. **Water**: Water work stimulates the dog's hunting instinct and is a more excitable environment.
6. **Distance**: The closer a dog is to you, the more influence you have over him. Distance from you acts as a distractor.
7. **Touch**: A person touching a dog creates a high level of distraction for that dog.
8. **Instinct**: The dog has some primary instincts that cause high distraction levels. The major one is hunting, which is the biggest obstacle and distractor in training a dog to perform whistle stopping and taking hand signals to an unseen fallen bird. We magnify the effect of instinct with some of the traditional retriever-training practices.
9. **Barometric pressure changes** affect a dog.
10. **Temperature changes** also affect a dog.

The key to training your dog to deal with distraction is to expose him to it gradually in a planned manner. Train the behavior to a level of 90 percent consistency in one location, and then, while using the same location, start introducing, sequentially and gradually, several distractions. Distance is one way to decrease the impact of a distraction. Start the dog with the distractor distant and then move it closer while keeping the dog successful at whatever the behavior is. When the dog is fluent in a behavior with a moderate level of distraction, move the training scenario to other locations.

For example, pick a one-acre area of short grass and train your dog to 90 percent proficiency in the behavior of sitting calmly for a dummy throw accompanied with a gunshot. Then have him perform the behavior as a kid walks past bouncing a basketball. Start with the kid walking past with the bouncing ball fifty feet away and your dog performing the behavior on leash. Next session, do it off leash. Third session, do it with your dog off leash and the kid bouncing the ball at thirty feet distant. Then bring it in to ten feet.

Next, still using the same location, add another dog doing some retrieves. When your dog is proficient at sitting still for falling dummies with gunshots and with other dogs retrieving at that first location, move to other locations. Each time you move to a new location, simplify the behavior. Thus, on location two, if the first performance with no distractions is good, then add back the kid with the basketball. The dog should quickly master this. Then add back the other dogs retrieving while your dog is performing.

The basic principles of positive training are quite simple. The difficult and critical part is the introduction and use of distraction. Training the dog to handle distraction is critical, whether it is positive training or whether it is traditional compulsion training. The key skill for the trainer is the ability to inject distraction gradually enough that the dog remains successful. It is important that distraction not be treated as a test, but rather as an element to be injected at a gradual enough rate of increase to keep the dog successful.

Whistle Stopping and Distraction

The most demanding gundog behaviors to be trained are whistle stopping and hand signals. Additionally, we make it a hundred times more difficult through the pursuit of a couple of traditional training practices. The first is to give a puppy many, many marked retrieves. We typically do this to "build drive," which is a fallacy, since the amount of drive in a dog is inherited from his parents. These marked retrieves, in effect, train the puppy to find the prey with no assistance from a trainer. The behavior chain is: go, hunt, reward. There is no whistle stop in that chain. Every marked retrieve trains the puppy to not stop on a whistle. Marked retrieves should be treated as a distraction and added into the training program after the dog is proficient on whistle stopping and blind retrieves.

The dog needs very little training to master the behavior of going to collect a bird that he has seen fall. It is a behavior he is born with. If his ancestors hundreds of years ago had been unable to go collect a bird that was seen to light in a distant field, then those ancestors died.

Another faulty training practice is working a puppy or young dog on birds too early and too much. Every bird the dog gets increases the distraction level of his already strong instinct to hunt. That instinct does not need any training. Whistle stops and directional casts need training. Establish the behaviors of whistle stopping and directional casts to a high level of fluency before bringing on the birds.

Typically we give a puppy lots of birds in the name of "building drive." Every bird you give to a young dog reinforces his propensity to hunt on his own and weakens his propensity to stop on a whistle and take a cast. He already has a built-in, genetic hunt drive. He inherited it from his parents. That inheritance cannot be made larger with birds. However, the more that inheritance is reinforced with high-value rewards like birds, the more difficult it is going to be to train the dog on whistle stops and hand signals to go where you want him to go. Birds should be looked at not as a drive-builder, but as a distraction to be added to a structured training program after the dog is proficient with steadiness and with whistle stopping and blind retrieves.

With some knowledge of distraction and its effect on the dog's performance, you should be able to do a better job of training. When the dog is not performing the way you want, try to identify the source of distraction and reduce it to a level the dog can handle. Then, gradually build it back up.

Alternatively, if you can't identify and reduce the distraction, then simplify the behavior that you are asking for and reduce it to a level the dog can accommodate. Either way, the solution lies in lowering your criteria to a level that the dog can perform and then gradually building back to the level you want.

That is the easy way to train a great dog that is flexible and able to handle new situations as they arise in the pursuit of his gundog job.

Training the Gundog: an Overview

The gundog's job is fairly clear-cut and easily defined. His job is to enhance your outdoors experience and provide treasured companionship. To do this, he has two job components:

1. **Be obedient, steady, and calm in high-distraction environments up to and including a hundred ducks circling the blind with six guns shooting.**

   The dog's basic purpose is to enhance your outdoors experience. You should be able to sit the dog in (or out of) the duck blind and be confident that he will remain where he is without further attention from you. That enables you to enjoy the hunting. Additionally, an overexcited, on-the-edge-of-control dog that is bouncing around in a duck blind full of loaded guns is flat dangerous. Whether the scenario is duck hunting, pheasant hunting, fly-fishing, or any other outdoor activity, a dog should be easily manageable and obedient so that you can confidently take him along with you, regardless of where it might be. This ability requires that the dog be well schooled in self-control.

2. **When the birds are down and there are several close, dead birds and one long unseen, crippled bird, the dog needs to fetch the long unseen cripple first.**

    The dog's supreme conservation contribution is to retrieve the crippled bird first. You don't want the crippled duck to swim off while the dog is retrieving the close, easy, dead ducks.

If you train the behaviors necessary for these two functions, you will have an excellent gundog.

START EARLY

Many traditional trainers preach waiting until six months of age to commence training. That is probably a wise adage if you are using the traditional training model of compulsion, which is based on "pressure" (a euphemism for force or punishment). When you are using positive training, puppies learn incredibly rapidly. Early puppy training in impulse control and operating in a distraction environment pay immense dividends over a dog's lifetime. The early training makes the later training very easy.

A TRAINING PLAN

Most projects in life are entered into with a plan. If the plan is written, the probability is much greater that the plan will succeed. Write a training plan for your dog. He is a ten- to twelve-year investment. You both will have a much richer journey if you conduct the higher-quality training program provided by a well-organized, written plan with time-phased objectives.

Keep notes of training sessions. Then you will know which behaviors are less fluent and need more reinforcement in future training sessions.

SEQUENCE OF BEHAVIORS

The sequence in which you train behaviors matters. The major area to be careful of is marked retrieves. Those are retrieves that the pup has seen fall. He needs nearly zero marked retrieves prior to becoming fluent on blind retrieves. The sequence of behaviors forms the skeleton of your training plan.

Here is a sequence of behaviors that I have found to produce excellent gundogs:

1. **Sitting**: this is most easily accomplished with place boards.
2. **Steady for falls**: this is most easily accomplished with place boards.
3. **Heeling**: first off leash, then on leash.
4. **Memory retrieves**: taking the pup with you to "plant the blind."
5. **Stop/Look on whistle**: this does not require sitting on the whistle.
6. **Long unseen cripple**: a chain of behavior built upon the prior behaviors.
7. **Marked retrieves**: The pup is born with the ability to accomplish marked retrieves. He does not need a lot of training on them other than building some confidence on distance.

CHAPTER 5

Gundog Behaviors: Innate and Trained

———————

MOST OF THE BEHAVIORS YOUR gundog needs he inherited from his ancestors. Most of the behaviors of all nature's creatures are inherited. Some examples are:

1. A robin's nest is a very distinctive cup shape with lots of mud and straw. They all look the same, whether the robin that makes it lives in Maine or Florida. Robins don't go to nest-building school to learn how to build it. Nest building is an inherited behavior.

2. Practically all the behaviors of a honeybee are inherited. Some of the honeybee's complex, innate behaviors are hive building, nectar gathering, and honey production and storage. Of amazing complexity is the honeybee's location dance. When a honeybee has found a field rich in pollen and nectar, she returns to the hive and performs a dance that communicates to the other bees the direction and distance to the field. These bee behaviors are the same regardless of geography. Note there is not a honeybee university teaching these skills.

3. A whelping bitch exhibits a complex set of behaviors. She expels her puppies. She nips and removes the fetal sac. She

nips the umbilical cord. She licks and cleans and dries the puppies.

She pushes away defective puppies based on a low body temperature. All bitches perform these behaviors and perform them the same way. They don't go to Lamaze class to learn it. It is a set of innate behaviors.

Sometimes humans cause an override in the whelping behavior sequence. When people make a bitch nervous by paying too much attention and bothering her, she will start picking up puppies in her mouth to try and move them to a new, safer location. This is another instinctive behavior.

Many of the behaviors your dog needs as a gundog are inherited. These innate behaviors need simply to be recognized, reinforced, and preserved. Here are the major gundog innate behaviors:

1. **Hunt**: Hunting is a primary instinctive behavior that the dog is born with. The trainer simply needs to let the dog's hunts succeed most of the time, especially during the puppy stage of life.
2. **Retrieve**: When a dog's ancestor saw a bird light in an opening across the field, that ancestral dog had the behavior set to stalk, catch, and eat that bird. Ancestral dogs that did not have that behavior set died. That same behavior set is the foundation of today's dog retrieving an object he has seen fall. Through selective breeding over the past several hundred years, we have greatly reinforced the part of the behavior chain that encompasses bringing the bird to the human's hand. If you throw a small, soft object ten to fifteen feet, a seven- to eight-week-old Labrador puppy will go get it and bring it back to you with no training, if you don't interfere with the behavior. Interference is usually generated by people and punishment. Here is an example. You give

the puppy ten retrieves every day. He starts experiencing fatigue and muscle burn at number five, but we have bred out the stop switch, so he keeps going through number ten. Fatigue and muscle burn feel bad to the puppy and hence are punishments. Punishment is cumulative. A number of small ones become the same as one big punishment. On the sixth day of this regimen, the puppy stops retrieving. You have exceeded his tolerance for punishment on this behavior and have suppressed the behavior. Obviously, these numbers are merely an example. Different dogs have different tolerance levels for various punishments.

3. **Carry**: All retrievers have an innate, behavioral tendency to carry stuff in their mouths. It is a product of selective breeding for several hundred years. With no interference, carrying will remain prominent in the pup's behavior set. As with the retrieving behavior, people have a great propensity to interfere with carrying behavior. For example, the puppy comes into the living room carrying your wife's Ferragamo shoe. You take the shoe, pop the puppy on the snout, and yell, "NO!" Two days later, you take the puppy out into the yard and throw him a dummy. He runs out to look at it but doesn't pick it up. He returns without the dummy. Of course, you have forgotten the punishment delivered four days ago for carrying the shoe. The puppy obviously has not. You did not intend to punish him for carrying a dummy, but the pup's behavior change tells you that you did. When the puppy brings you something, regardless of what it is, the appropriate response is few strokes on the head, a "good dog" or two, and thanks for the nice delivery to hand.

4. **Deliver to hand**: As with carrying, all retrievers have delivery to hand as an innate behavior, or, until forty years ago, all retrievers used to. With the widespread practice of force fetch in the United States, the ability to observe, measure,

and selectively breed for that particular behavioral trait is greatly hampered. In the United Kingdom gene pool, the trait is almost 100 percent present in the field-bred Labrador. When delivery-to-hand problems are encountered with a puppy, the cause is generally punishment.

Suppose on a Monday you accidently step on the pup's foot, and he yelps in pain and jumps away. You are talking to a neighbor and don't take much notice. Two days later, you take the puppy out into the yard and throw him a dummy. He runs out to it, grabs in, and brings it back toward you. As he approaches, he hesitates, drops the dummy about three feet away, and then comes to you. That punishment you unintentionally and accidentally delivered to him two days prior established a punishment zone around you.

I once had a trainer who came to me and told me that one of her puppies, in spite of previous good performance, had quit going into his crate on cue. "Show me," I said.

The trainer, with the puppy accompanying her, walked over, sat the puppy, opened the crate, and said, "Kennel." The puppy remained sitting in front of the crate. Several more attempts brought the same nonresponse.

I said, "Leave the puppy sitting at the crate, and leave the crate door open. Step four feet away from the crate, and cue the puppy again 'kennel.'"

She did, and the puppy went right into the crate.

The trainer had created around herself a small punishment zone that extended past the door of the crate. Moving the trainer moved the zone and "unblocked" the entry into the crate.

5. **Chase:** It is an innate response to chase prey running away. It also is triggered by other puppies running away or by a human running or walking away. A walking human is moving at a puppy's running speed. If a puppy is distracted and

not coming to you, all you have to do is keep your mouth shut and walk away. Keep walking until the puppy realizes he is alone. Many humans interpret this to mean walk ten feet, turn, stop, and shout, jump up and down, etc. To the puppy, those behaviors are simply rewards for not coming. The valid prompt (trigger) to get the pup coming is the person walking silently away. Then, when the pup finally realizes you have departed and he is getting no audible broadcasts on your location, he will put his extraordinary nose to work and come find you. When he finds you, give him a big reward (edible is more valuable to the pup).

6. **Tracking**: Just as the pup will automatically track you down upon a silent departure, so will he track down a crippled bird. It is an innate behavior. All you need to do is make sure that the first couple of experiences are simple enough for him to succeed.

7. **Herding**: Herding behavior was a survival requirement for the dog's ancestor, the gray wolf. In times of low availability of small game, the ancient gray wolf, for survival, had to pull down larger game. To accomplish this feat frequently required several wolves working together to corner and kill the animal. Thus, it required herding behavior. Dogs today retain remnants of that herding behavior. That also means that they have a talent for responding to human changes of direction of travel. That matters in teaching hand signals.

If you preserve the dog's innate behaviors, you don't have to train a lot of others. Your training needs to be focused on training his self-control and on developing his abilities to go out under directional control to find and fetch the birds he didn't see fall.

CHAPTER 6

Punishment and Unwanted Behaviors

———

THE MAJOR USE OF PUNISHMENT is to eliminate unwanted behaviors. Punishment does work in extinguishing unwanted behavior if it is applied within seconds of that behavior. Otherwise, it works to extinguish whatever behavior was occurring when or just before the punishment arrived. The classic example of poorly timed punishment occurs when an unwanted behavior occurs thirty yards away from the trainer, and the trainer calls the dog to him and punishes the dog. That punishment will tend to extinguish the dog's behavior of coming to the trainer.

Punishment also carries some other notable results. Punishment usually causes the dog to avoid the location where he was punished. That includes the trainer. When the dog is close to the trainer and experiences a punishment, the dog will avoid the trainer. This trainer avoidance is one of the major causes of failure of a puppy's natural behavior of delivery to hand.

Examples include a person punishing a puppy on Monday for carrying a shoe in his mouth, or a person accidently stepping on the puppy's foot on Monday. Then, on Wednesday, the person throws a dummy for the puppy. The puppy runs out, picks up the dummy, and runs most of the way back, but slows when he arrives close to the person and spits out the dummy. The person encourages him to come on, and the puppy comes on to him. The dummy remains where it dropped. The hesitation on final approach and the dropping of the dummy are the result of the avoidance response implanted by the punishment on Monday. It doesn't matter whether the punishment was intentional or unintentional; it was a punishment. It happened right next to the person. It caused the formation of an avoidance response relative to that person.

Another example might be if a person on Monday is drying dishes, and he drops a dishcloth. The puppy grabs it. The person whacks the puppy on the snout, makes a threatening noise, and takes the dishcloth. On Wednesday, the person tosses a retrieving dummy for the puppy. He runs out almost to it, stops, and returns without the dummy. The punishment has stopped his retrieving.

The obvious solution is to not punish puppies around retrieving. However, if you do deliver a punishment in close proximity to you, either accidentally or on purpose, you have about ten minutes to mitigate the avoidance response.

Studies with rats have indicated that when an animal undergoes a fearful experience, there is a short, following time period during which the animal's fear response can be modified. There is an approximate ten-minute delay before the fearful response processes into long-term memory. Thus, the trainer has only a brief time period to change the animal's response.

The trainer should use this grace period. Whenever you deliver a punishment to a dog close to you, whether it is accidental or whether it is intentional, counteract the unwanted effects. Wait a brief time, and then pet the dog, pull him close to you, pet him, and give him a treat to counteract the avoidance part of his response. If it involves a puppy and retrieving or delivery to hand, give him a couple of short, playful retrieves.

To punish correctly and effectively requires a higher skill level on the part of the trainer—the skill level that comes from training twenty or forty or sixty or one hundred dogs. Most sportsmen will not train that many dogs in a lifetime. Most sportsmen will have a higher probability of successfully training their dog if they minimize the punishment element.

Unwanted Behavior

Through decades of dog training, my experience has proven to me that adopting the positive-training model increases the probability by at least 300 percent of a beginning trainer turning out an excellent gundog.

All that it requires is a little knowledge and a change in perspective. Look at unwanted behavior as something to remain unpaid and something to be prevented by strengthening a competing behavior.

A great example is a dog that jumps up and paws you—a very common problem that most people deal with by looking at the dog, making noises, and pushing on the dog. If you look at that scenario from a positive-training perspective, the person is rewarding the dog with the person's behavior. His looking at the dog gives the dog attention. He is making noises, which, again, give attention. He is pushing on the dog, which is play to the dog, which is a reward.

The best way to deal with the jumping-up behavior is to reinforce a competing behavior. Give a lot of payments for sitting and for approaching a person and sitting. In a couple of days, you can have a dog who automatically makes the decision and sits upon approaching a person.

All unwanted behaviors can be dealt with in that manner. If the dog is engaging in unwanted behavior at a distance, ramp up payments for coming and also for coming in the face of distraction. If the dog is refusing whistles at a distance, ramp up payments for whistle stops at a distance, including whistle stops with distraction. If the dog is making noise, ramp up payments for being quiet.

CHAPTER 7

Communication: You Said What?

———————

COMMUNICATION IS NEARLY NEVER MENTIONED in discussions of dog training. Communication, however, is the most important piece of the puzzle. How do you tell the dog what you want him to do? A quite typical approach is to speak English to the dog and see if he will respond. This does not work. A look at how dogs communicate will furnish a better model.

The dog communicates almost exclusively with his eyes and body language. To take in information from another dog, he reads body posture, body motion, direction of motion, eye movements, tail movements, ear movements, etc. When a dog gives information to another dog, he does it with the same mechanisms. He moves, changes his posture, repositions his ears, looks in the direction he is going to go, etc. A prime example is that of a person taking a group of six or eight dogs on a hike. During the hike, the dogs will engage in lots of group activities, play, hunting, etc. There will be loads of communication going on between the dogs. Not a sound will be heard other than the rattle of leaves and bushes stirred by busy paws.

A great example of dog communicating with man is the dog that knows when you get ready to go hunting. That dog reacts well before you get your gun or gear. The human thinks the dog is reading his mind. The dog is actually reading the owner's eyes. The owner looks toward the gun cabinet, or he looks toward the closet where his hunting coat hangs. The owner frequently doesn't notice the dog looking at him, because the dog has much greater scope of his peripheral vision. Humans have a field of view of about 180 degrees, while dogs, with their slightly offset eyes, can see about 270 degrees. The dog looks at the man much more frequently than the man comprehends.

Compared to the dog, man's interspecies communications skills frequently leave something to be desired. The human frequently stands still, which gives the dog nothing to read. Then the human starts making vocal noises. Words give the dog no useful information except when they are yelled angrily. In that case, the dog receives the information that says it would be wise to stay away from this angry, threatening person.

So how does the trainer communicate with the dog? The trainer keeps his mouth shut, keeps his body moving, and keeps his hands off the dog. One of the most valuable communication tools that I have found is a piece of duct tape. Place it across your mouth, and your training will improve tremendously. That is probably a little extreme, but it does illustrate the importance of keeping your voice out of the training process sufficiently to minimize interference. The main result of silence is that it influences the human to reach into his ancestral suite of behaviors and offer some nonverbal communication. We humans were around thousands of years prior to the point in history when speech emerged. We have buried in our brain stem those ancient talents and proclivities. When the trainer keeps his mouth shut, his innate talents have an opportunity to operate.

One of the most misunderstood communications is that of getting the dog to come to you. The human frequently stands still and yells at the dog, "Here! HERE!!! HERE!!!!!" If you want the dog to come to you, simply walk away from him and keep walking until he catches up. One of the first lessons I teach my new trainers is that "walk away from the dog" means keep walking until the dog catches up. It does not mean walk ten feet and stop, or walk twenty feet and stop. If you continue walking away and being quiet, in a few seconds the dog looks around and sees that you are gone. He doesn't know where you are, because you are being silent. Therefore, because he doesn't want to stay there by himself, he comes to find you. Initially, the distance may be ten feet, or it may be fifty yards. The dog determines what the distance is—not the trainer. The first lesson or two, you might have to walk thirty or forty yards before the dog "finds" you. By the third or fourth lesson, you will be walking maybe three or four steps before the dog "finds" you.

One of the most effective dog-training strategies is to use the voice very sparingly, and usually at a low volume. If you watch a few dog trainers, you will note that the good ones use very little noise.

That is not to say that the voice doesn't have a role in dog training. Voice is useful in training. It serves well as a marker for desired behaviors. "Good" in an upbeat tone can tell the dog that he is doing it right. "No" in a harsh tone can tell him he is doing it wrong. The vocal marker "good" is merely a sound and will only have value if followed frequently by a reward. Two typical high-value rewards are treats and retrieves. Petting and praise are typically medium- to low-value rewards, depending upon how indiscriminately they are bestowed during the pup's average day.

Reward, if properly used, is the most powerful communication channel with a dog. When the dog does what you want, reward him immediately for the behavior or mark it with a sound when the payment will be slightly delayed. That is the essence of good communication with animals.

CHAPTER 8

Cues, Commands, and Prompts

———

A CUE IS NOT A command. Commands are not commands either. Words do not produce behavior. A cue is a signal to the dog that he will get paid for performing a certain behavior. The cue does not produce the behavior. The behavior is produced by the previous week of sessions with many payments for many repetitions of the behavior. To put the behavior on cue, you gradually start preceding the behavior with the cue. Then you begin paying only the repetitions that are preceded by the cue. You stop paying the behavior when it is not preceded by the cue.

CUES

In the retriever-training world, a cue is a trigger to elicit a trained behavior from a dog. Many refer to a cue as a command. We make a very large assumption when we assume that the dog is picking the same cue that we are using for a particular behavior. When the trainer says, "Sit," and the dog sits, is the dog reacting to the sound of "sit," or is he reacting to a visual signal—a consistent movement, probably subconscious, that the trainer makes whenever the trainer says, "Sit"?

Consider the fact that dogs communicate almost entirely with the visual signals of a person's body language. In training, dogs preferentially pick a visual cue from the trainer to respond to. Frequently, this cue is not the word or sound emanating from the trainer's mouth. The dog is really responding to some body movement that the trainer has habitually and subconsciously accompanied with the verbal signal.

Also consider the dog's fourteen thousand years of evolution through domestication. Recent research suggests that early humans selected dogs for domestication by picking those animals more attuned to human communicative signals. Research demonstrates that dogs significantly read human behioral characteristics as subtle as eye movements in the communication process. These factors indicate that dogs prefer a visual to an auditory cue. When you say, "Sit," and the dog sits, he is more likely to be responding to your eye movements, or your infinitesimal head movement, or your slight posture change, than he is to your sound.

Trainer Kathy Sdao gave a great example of this tendency during a recent Clicker Expo. A prominent agility trainer and handler had a very talented dog that looked like a sure winner for the national competition. The dog had won several regional contests. At the national the dog started well and then froze at the first turn. He was unable to take a simple directional cue. He was out.

After the competition, an analysis of his failure determined that the freezing was caused by the absence of the handler's ponytail. The handler usually wore her hair pulled back in a ponytail and subconsciously accompanied her directional cues with a head movement that tossed her ponytail. For the regional competition, she had dressed more formally and had put her hair up. No ponytail. The dog was unable to respond, because the cue that the dog had selected and learned was not present.

The most important characteristics of a cue are that it be clear and distinct. If you are not aware of what cue or cues the dog is selecting, then the chore of making that cue or cues separate and distinct becomes quite difficult.

To add more confusion, here is a piece of Pavlov's research, which I came across recently in *Fundamentals of Learning and Motivation* by Frank Logan.

EXPERIMENTAL NEUROSIS

One use of the procedure of differentials in classical conditioning is to determine how fine a discrimination an animal is capable of. With humans, of course, we can simply ask whether two tones sound alike or different, but with animals, we need to develop some nonverbal response by which they can communicate to the experimenter. Clearly, if an animal can learn to respond differentially to two stimuli (cues), he can discriminate between them.

In an effort to obtain such information, Pavlov would first employ differential conditioning with stimuli (cues) that were quite dissimilar; say, a very high-pitched tone versus a very low-pitched tone. He would then make them progressively more similar in an attempt to find out where the discrimination broke down indicating that the animal could no longer respond differentially. Interestingly enough, he found that when the stimuli (cues) became very similar, not only did the discrimination break down, so did the dog!

The dog would show obvious signs of fear and anxiety about the experimental situation, so that rather than standing quietly in the stock and salivating when appropriate, he would resist the situation. This behavior carried over to his total behavior. He would huddle in a corner of his living cage, cower at the sight of his familiar handler, refuse to eat regularly, and overreact to the slightest sound or distraction.

Pavlov called this result an experimental neurosis because of its apparent similarity to many human neurotic behaviors, and he usually had to send the dog away from the laboratory for a rest cure of tender care in the country.

Considering all the above factors, it appears that is important to pick cues that are separate and distinct and to use those cues in a well-defined manner. All of this should also tell you that it is quite important for the puppy to be trained by only one person. No two people have the same body language, so no matter what the word is that is emanating from the human mouth, two different people are going to be sending two different signals in terms of body language. Pavlov's experiment demonstrates that lack of consistency of cues has the potential to cause some problems.

You will greatly enhance your if you occasionally check to see what cue the dog is using. Try training with your mouth shut. Give no verbal cues, only gestures. Try it with sunglasses on. That will disguise your eye movements. Try it sitting down instead of standing. You might be surprised to see how often the dog is responding to a signal other than your words.

Because fuzzy cues make it much harder for the dog to behave as desired, it is unwise to have two different trainers during the dog's active learning periods. He will survive it. He will probably even learn in spite of the trainer because of his flexibility, but the learning process will be much more difficult for the dog.

As no two people use the same body language, a dog with two trainers will get inconsistent cues. That is not a recipe for success.

PROMPTS

A prompt is an enabler or trigger for a behavior. One example in dog training is a raised-hand, "traffic cop" gesture to induce a dog to stay. A trainer uses the prompt to produce behavior so he can reinforce it. As the behavior is becoming established, the trainer fades the prompt and continues the reinforcement.

Another useful prompt is walking decisively in the direction you want the dog to go when giving a directional cast. The dog has an innate propensity to herd as a legacy from his wolf ancestors. When wolves need to kill a large animal, they must operate jointly to bring it down. This joint behavior is basically herding. In the dog, it manifests itself in the dog moving the direction that he sees the trainer move.

The first few times the dog is given a directional cast, the trainer should take three or four or five decisive steps in the desired direction. Then, as the dog gains proficiency on directional casts, the prompting steps are faded from five to four to one to one-half. The reward comes from the dummy or bird found at the end of the cast or casts.

CHAPTER 9

Delivery to Hand

———

WHEN DEALING WITH A HIGH percentage of cripples such as produced by the author when shooting steel shot, a bird in the hand is worth two dropped at your feet. A duckdog needs to deliver to hand. Your dog's delivery to hand of birds is a conservation feature. When he drops a crippled duck just shy of the blind, he is usually in for a lengthy chase-and-recapture event that might not succeed. A similar result can occur with upland hunting when, after a lengthy hunting-and-trailing process, a dog fetches back a lively cock pheasant and drops it five feet away from you. Another lengthy hunt is likely to occur, and you again might lose the bird. Dropped cripples and repeat performances result in time lost from hunting and an increased number of birds not recaptured.

The solution is to train the dog to reliably deliver to hand. If you are starting with a puppy, that project should be fairly easy. Labradors have been selectively bred for the past 170 years to naturally deliver to hand. All the trainer needs to do is preserve that ability.

PRESERVING NATURAL DELIVERY TO HAND

To preserve delivery to hand, you simply keep the pup wanting to come to you. This feat is fairly simply done by rewarding him frequently with treats for the act of coming to you. Past that, you merely avoid doing things that cause the puppy to spit out a dummy. The major culprits for erasing delivery to hand in puppies are:

1. Standing up straight and stiffly as a puppy is arriving with a dummy. That posture is threatening to a small puppy. It makes it difficult for him to approach you. Go down on one knee as the pup approaches and put your hands down below the level of his head to receive the dummy. Slip your hands under his jaw and support it while he holds the dummy for a second or two and while you stroke him gently on his head. Then, take the dummy.

2. Don't step toward the puppy as he arrives with the dummy. A puppy has an innate response to retreat from an advancing, large animal such as a person. The prelude to the retreat is spitting out the dummy.

3. Don't reach down from over his head to take the dummy. A puppy has an innate response to duck away from a threat descending from above. This trait helps protect him from airborne predators. If you reach down from above, he will probably duck away, spitting out the dummy in the process.

4. Don't hurt or frighten the puppy in close proximity to the trainer. This scenario creates a punishment zone around the trainer, making it difficult for the puppy to make the final approach to the trainer. As the puppy approaches the edge of the punishment zone (about three feet), he spits out the dummy. A loud voice can create a punishment zone for a sensitive puppy. Jerking on his neck with the leash for heeling can cause a punishment zone. Any punishment delivered to a puppy in close proximity to the trainer can inadvertently create a punishment zone. It can happen if you punish the puppy for chewing on your wife's best shoes or on your favorite duck call. The punishment delivery creates the zone. The "why" of the punishment is not relevant.

FIXING BOTCHED NATURAL DELIVERY TO HAND

You may have gotten a pup from parents who did not transmit the necessary genes for their puppies to naturally deliver to hand. You may have failed in your effort to preserve delivery to hand by inadvertently "poisoning" the puppy's delivery-to-hand behavior. Either way, the solution is to train the pup to fetch an object from the ground on getting a signal from you. There are two ways to train this behavior: the easy way and the hard way.

FORCE FETCH

The hard way to train the fetch from ground behavior is the traditional force-fetch process, in which you use an ear pinch or toe pinch to compel the dog to fetch an object from the ground. This force process takes a good bit of training skill, and the process may take four to eight weeks to complete. It is not fun for the dog, nor is it fun for the trainer.

THE TENNIS BALL GAME

The easy way to train the fetch-from-ground behavior is the tennis ball game. You have all seen this game played in reverse. Everyone has been at a friend's house, sitting in a chair, and experienced the family dog approaching and nudging you on the leg. You reach down and take the ball the dog is holding as he nudges your leg. You toss the ball for the dog to retrieve. That dog has trained humans to toss a ball from him by delivering the ball to the person's hand. From a different perspective, you could say that the dog has trained himself to deliver to hand by discovering that a person will reward with a toss of the ball delivered to hand. If the dog can accidentally train himself to deliver to hand in order to get a throw, then humans should be able to make it happen by design.

Absolutely Positively Gundog Training

The great thing about the tennis ball game is that in addition to the dog being able to learn it, the game is easy for people to play as well. Here are the steps:

1. Take the dog into a room. Shut the door so that there is no place to go except back to you. Use this room until the behavior is well established.

2. Give him a couple of retrieves of a bouncing tennis ball with a playful cue of "Fetch." When he brings the ball to hand, give him a short toss. If he does not come to you, stop the game and work on reinforcing "Come" with treats for a couple of days; then, resume the tennis ball game. Each time he delivers to hand, pay with a toss. If he drops the ball next to you and doesn't pick it back up, end the game. One or two sessions should have him fetching a bouncing ball.

3. For session two, simply roll the ball across the floor and say, "Fetch." When he fetches it to hand, pay him with a toss. Repeat three or four times. Then, roll very slowly and say, "Fetch." When he fetches to hand, pay him with a toss. Repeat three or four times. Then, place the ball on the floor and leave it still for a few seconds, and cue the pup with, "Fetch." When he delivers to hand, pay with a toss.

4. For session three, cue the pup once with, "Fetch," on a rolling tennis ball, and then twice on a stationary ball. For each delivery to hand, pay with a toss. For the fourth or fifth fetch session, drop a small, canvas dummy on the floor and cue with, "Fetch." When he fetches the dummy and delivers to hand, pay him with a toss of the tennis ball. You might need to bump the dummy with your toe initially to give it a little motion. Then cue with "Fetch," and pay the delivery to hand with the tennis ball toss. The tennis ball is a higher-value reward to most dogs. Repeat three or four times and stop.

61

5. The next step is the fetch-the-dummy-pay-with-tennis-ball drill in another room in the house, then in the yard a few times, and then to the field. When the dog is proficient at fetching on cue a dummy from the ground in most field conditions, try him on birds.

The whole process can be done in about ten sessions over the course of a week. This time will be very well spent and will greatly add to the conservation value of your retriever, because a bird in the hand is worth two birds dropped at your feet.

You can see a short video of the process here: http://www.youtube.com/watch?v=BrOkq9fsSkI

Or go to http://www.youtube.com and input the title: "Paying fetch from ground with tennis ball toss—Buccleuch Temperance"

CHAPTER 10

Place Boards and Steadiness

———

WHEN A WILD COYOTE FINDS a section of stream where trout congregate and catches a few there, he remembers it. That coyote has an internal navigation system that will bring him back to that same place in the future when he is hungry. The same phenomenon occurs with a wolf who encounters a thicket well populated with rabbits. All animals have an internal navigation system that will take them back to the spot where they found food. This propensity to be attracted to the specific location at which a reward occurred is the underlying principle for place board training.

The place boards we use are of one-quarter-inch plywood and measure about eighteen inches by eighteen inches. The dimensions are not critical, nor is the material. The important facets of a place board are that it be easily portable and that it be of a size that a gundog can sit comfortably on. I use plywood because it is fairly durable and not unduly slippery. A rubber mat works equally well.

I use place boards for training the initial behaviors of sitting and staying for the dog. The place board makes the training process easier for the dog and for the trainer. These lessons are the puppy's initial training in self-control and the foundation for a calm, steady, obedient companion and gundog in the future.

The Place Board Training Process

The place board serves as a magnet for the dog. The more rewards a puppy gets on the place board, the more he wants to be on it. Thus, the place board also helps prompt certain behaviors in an otherwise distractive or new environment. An example would be going to a new training area with higher distraction levels (such as other dogs or people moving around). Perhaps you have come here to continue your dog's training on the long unseen cripple exercise, and you find that the dog's behaviors of coming and delivery to hand start failing due to the high distraction levels. The dog does fine on the whistle stops and casts and makes a nice retrieve, but you have trouble getting him all the way back to you for the delivery to hand.

Bring out the place board. Put it on the ground and stand beside it. If the dog has had the proper introductory conditioning on the place board, it will frequently overcome his distraction issues, and he will smoothly come to you and deliver to hand. That will turn a poor training session into a good one.

Place boards also give the trainer and the dog a more structured scenario so that the training exercise is better defined for both.

On the initial place board training, I suggest not using the clicker. You will be right next to the puppy. Thus, distance from the puppy is not an issue for correct timing. You don't need a marker. You can deliver the treat in a timely fashion upon completion of the behavior with reduced probability of trainer mistakes. Doing a little work without the clicker will also give you a better grasp of the fact that the reward, not the click, is what changes the dog's behavior.

Whenever you encounter difficulty, you are probably trying to go too fast or asking for too large a measure of improvement. The solution is to back up a couple of sessions and then move forward again in smaller steps. The objective is to always have the pup succeed. Human nature sometimes makes that difficult. Most of us have a strong tendency to test the pup frequently to see if he can go a little faster. Keep that human fault in check, and your training will go smoothly and rapidly.

Adjust the number of sessions to the rate of progress the puppy makes. That progress will vary from puppy to puppy and from trainer to trainer. A good rule of thumb is to limit sessions to three minutes and do no more than one per day. Puppies are easy to overwork from both a physical standpoint and a mental-capacity perspective. Humans tend to get occasionally stubborn and work far too long on a particular exercise. If you find yourself getting involved in long, unproductive training sessions, get a timer that rings a bell at three minutes. Use it.

If you are quiet while training, you will find that the puppy will progress more rapidly. Your voice simply raises the distraction level and makes learning more difficult for the puppy. Save the voice until the behavior is fluent, and then use the voice as a distraction to begin the process of distraction proofing.

The behaviors of sitting and staying are excellent for this initial use of the place board. Here is a typical scenario with a twelve-week-old puppy. You may need to adjust it to fit your puppy.

You will have to make some judgments on length of sessions and on when your puppy is ready to progress to the next level. It is better to err to the conservative side.

The behavior sequence and lesson plan is:

1. Objective: the puppy sits on the place board.
    *   Holding a treat several inches above the pup's head, lure him onto the place board. Pay a few times for "four feet on the board." Then, start holding the treat high enough above his head that he looks up. Pay for the "look up." Then, gradually expand the time that he looks up before you pay. After several payments, the pup will relieve the

strain on his neck muscles by sitting to look up and get the payment.

- Over several sessions, the pup will be sitting quite promptly on a place board. He should also be sitting in a relaxed manner as opposed to a "crouch."

2. Objective: the puppy sits on the place board a longer time.
    - Hold a treat several inches above the pup's head and wait for him to sit. Repeat several times.
    - When the pup is sitting promptly at the sight of the hand above his head, start delaying the payments for a half second, then a second, and then two seconds.

3. Objective: the puppy sits on the place board for fifteen seconds.
    - This exercise takes trainer motor skills, so first practice your fast delivery of treats. Put a cup on the place board and practice reaching in the treat pouch, picking a treat, and delivering it as fast as you can. This is a barrage of payments. When you are fast with the cup, get the pup.
    - Start with barrage payments for sitting. When the pup sits, start paying with treats rapidly enough that he doesn't have a chance to get up. Pay ten treats successively without him getting up. Then, lure him off the board and back on and repeat the barrage payment.
    - Then repeat the ten-successive-treats barrage as above.
    - Then sit the pup on the place board, wait one-half second, and pay. Gradually, over a couple of training sessions, build from one-half second, to one second, to two seconds, and up to fifteen seconds.
    - A puppy fails to hold a sit because he is trying to get to the treat source, which is you. A few barrages of treats as above will allow him to relax in the expectation of getting more treats shortly. This practice leads to a puppy

that sits in a relaxed manner. The puppy learns that sitting pays more than getting up pays. This training is the cornerstone of impulse control and the foundation upon which is built the behavior of staying calm in a high-distraction environment.

4. Objective: The puppy sits on the place board while the trainer backs away two steps and returns. This behavior will start with a ten-second sit and progress to a sit with another distraction parameter, that of the trainer moving away.

   • The trainer should perform this session walking in place instead of standing still. On several repetitions toward the end, the trainer will step quickly away and back to the puppy and pay. The trainer's movement should be so fast that the puppy doesn't have a chance to get up. The puppy does not want you to move away, because you are the treat machine. You move back quickly so that the pup discovers that payment is coming even though you have moved away a step.

   • Sit the pup on the board; pay three or four treats rapidly so that he stays sitting.

   • Sit the pup on the board; wait three seconds and then pay.

   • Sit the pup on the board; wait five seconds and then pay.

   • Sit the pup on the board; wait eight seconds and then pay.

   • Sit the pup on the board; wait ten seconds and then pay.

   • Sit the pup on the board; step one step rapidly away and just as quickly back to the pup. The rapid step away and then back is to teach him that you are not leaving. You can fade the speedy stepping gradually to slow steps, and then to walking away and pausing for a gradually longer time before returning to pay.

- With the pup sitting on the place board, rapidly step two steps away and return and pay. Repeat this several times while decreasing the speed of stepping away at returning and paying. Repeat the two-steps-away exercise three times.

5. Objective: The puppy sits on the place board while the trainer turns 180 degrees and moves two steps away. The trainer should be walking in place during this exercise.
   - Sit the puppy on the place board and pay five treats rapidly while the pup remains sitting.
   - Sit the puppy on the place board; wait one second and pay.
   - Sit the puppy on the place board; delay four seconds and pay.
   - Sit the puppy on the place board; delay six seconds and pay.
   - Sit the puppy on the place board; turn quickly left ninety degrees and then quickly turn back and pay.
   - Sit the puppy on the place board; turn quickly right ninety degrees and then quickly turn back and pay
   - Sit the puppy on the place board. Turn quickly 180 degrees. Take one step quickly away and then quickly return and pay.
   - Sit the puppy on the place board. Turn quickly 180 degrees. Take two steps quickly away and then quickly return and pay.
   - Sit the puppy on the place board. Turn quickly 180 degrees. Take one step quickly away and then quickly return and pay.
   - Do several repetitions of the pup staying, while you step away and return more slowly.

Gradually, over the next few sessions, lengthen the time the pup remains sitting and also lengthen the distance the trainer moves away. After the pup is proficient at sitting calmly while the trainer turns and walks quickly away for ten feet and pauses for ten to twenty seconds before returning to pay, it is time to move the drill to a new location and add some variations. The most important variation is to reinforce the behavior of sitting calmly in the face of increasing distraction. The major distractor to tackle will be that of falls of retrievable objects. The next step will be steadiness.

STEADINESS FOR FALLS

The gundog's job is fairly clear-cut and easily defined. His job is to enhance your outdoors experience and provide treasured companionship. The gundog piece of this has two job components:

1. Be obedient and calm in a high-distraction environment up to and including one hundred ducks circling the blind with six guns shooting.
2. When the birds are down and there are several close dead birds and one long unseen cripple bird, the dog needs to fetch the long unseen cripple first.

If you train the behaviors necessary for these two functions, you will have an excellent gundog and a dog that can adapt readily to any outdoors endeavor.

Your training program should have two tracks: the <u>steadiness</u> track and the <u>blinds-and-hand-signals</u> track. You initially will keep the two tracks separate and distinct; after a few weeks, start blending them together. "Separate and distinct" means you conduct the sessions from track one in a different place than track two. Lessons should be short (three to five minutes) and no more frequent than once per day. Every other day is better for the dog, but daily keeps it easier for the human portion of the team.

The steadiness track begins with place board training and continues with increasing distraction-proofing—the behavior objective is sitting calmly in a high-distraction environment. Place boards make this behavior much easier for the dog.

If your dog or puppy has regularly been required to wait before going to fetch a retrieve, this series of lessons will be fairly easy. If he has had lots and lots of unrestrained retrieves, then his impulse control will be poor and the training will be more difficult

The crux of the use of the guideline is that it must be geared to your dog. Each lesson must be looked at from the perspective of the dog's performance. You are looking for proficiency, not a certain number of lessons. This steadiness track, if performed properly, will pay tremendous dividends down the road. With it, you are basically developing the dog's impulse control, his self-control. In essence, the dog is learning that self-control pays better than hyperactivity.

You will use the clicker here to serve as a bridge for a switch of reward for the behavior of sitting calmly. You will change from a treat reward to a retrieve reward. Thus you will be using the high value reward of a retrieve to pay the dog for sitting calmly in the face of high distraction.

The steadiness is simply an extension of place board training. Start with a pup that has mastered sitting calmly on the place board while the trainer walks away six feet. This is a continuation of the previous place board training process described earlier.

The following sequence should occur over one to two sessions, depending on your skill level and on the nature and proper preparation of your puppy. Sit the pup on a place board for the exercise.

Here is the lesson in detail:

1. Sit the pup on the place board and give him eight to ten repetitions of a click immediately followed by a treat.
2. Walk away two steps, return, and click/treat.

3. Walk away two steps, pause and click, return, and pay.
4. Walk away six feet, stop and slowly wave the dummy, and then return and click/treat.
5. Walk away six feet, stop and more rapidly wave the dummy, and then return and click/treat.
6. Walk away six feet, stop and drop the dummy by your feet and pick it up, and then return, and click/treat.
7. Walk away six feet; stop and toss the dummy three feet away from you and away from the pup. Step over and pick up the dummy; return and click/treat.
8. Walk away six feet; stop and toss the dummy six feet from you and away from the pup. Pause one or two seconds. Click and gesture for the pup to fetch the dummy. This is the switch from treat to retrieve for the reward for sitting calmly for the fall.
9. Walk away six feet and toss the dummy six feet away from you and away from the pup. Then step over, pick it up, walk back to the pup, and click/treat.

Repeat the above exercise several times over several days, gradually moving farther away from him and giving more loft and distance to the throws. Then the pup will be ready to progress to the long unseen cripple drill. Pick up yourself three falls for every "payment." The act of the trainer picking up three out of four retrieves puts the retrieve reward on a variable schedule of reinforcement. When you reach this phase, the pup is well on his way to becoming a calm, steady, retrieving companion.

From here on, you should be careful about sending the pup quickly on marked retrieves. His brain chemistry is such that the sight of and expectation of retrieving a fallen bird or dummy gets him excited. The fall induces the release in his brain stem of neurochemicals such as adrenaline, endorphins, and dopamine. These chemicals produce a "buzz" that is a high-value reward to the dog. For a dog that has a history of instant gratification of being released or sent quickly for a number of falls, three minutes is the approximate time period for dissipation of the "excitement neurochemicals" so that the dog enters a calm emotional state. You can measure that excitement time by letting the dog watch a fall and restraining him. Offer him a treat every few seconds. He will show no interest in it as long as he is excited. When he calms, he will take the treat.

Pups that have had few marked retrieves and who have also been required to wait ten to sixty seconds before release for these retrieves will be a good bit calmer. The majority will have a dissipation time for those excitement brain chemicals that will be closer to fifteen or twenty seconds.

The next phase of training will be the long unseen cripple exercise. To begin that exercise, the pup must be able to sit calmly while you walk out thirty to forty feet from him, stop, and throw two marked falls for him.

CHAPTER 11

Long Unseen Cripple

AFTER 9/11, I WAS TASKED to rebuild a FEMA disaster-search dog program in need of reworking. To begin, I recruited fifteen dog handlers, of whom more than 50 percent were police and firefighters so that we got an emergency-response culture. Then I bought young, adult Labrador retrievers and placed one with each handler. The dog lived with and was trained by his handler. I trained the handlers to train the dogs. I had them two to three sessions per week for two or three hours.

I started off with traditional, compulsion training, which was all that I knew at that time. After about three months, I looked at our progress records and determined that at the rate we were going, it was going to take eighteen months to get the team operational. In the world of emergency operations, that is way too long. I had to find a faster training model. I looked around for a leading-edge, animal training program and found the US Navy's Marine Mammal Training program. They were training dolphins to detect tethered antisubmarine mines several hundred feet beneath the ocean's surface. The dolphins also had to conduct their searches through and around schools of fish. Since fish is their natural diet and also serves as the dolphins' training rewards, the behavior being trained was very difficult. They are trained entirely with B. F. Skinner's operant conditioning with positive reinforcement. I picked it for my search team.

The dog adaptation of B. F. Skinner's positive-training model is popularly termed "clicker training." I adopted it and started training dogs and handlers to the new model. I loaded all the handlers on an airplane, and we attended a national, three-day, clicker-training seminar consisting of presentations from world-class experts. I also followed up by bringing in two of these experts to conduct individual coaching with the handlers. The end result was the drastic reduction of the dog/handler training time. It went from eighteen months to six months, a 300 percent reduction. That told me the positive-training model is three times easier for novice trainers to master.

I have spent the past ten years developing a training model that adapts the B. F. Skinner positive-training model to retriever gundogs, and I have come up with a very simple, workable model. I have used it on over one hundred gundogs very successfully and have been teaching it to novice trainers with great success.

For a high probability of success with the training model, there are two prerequisites:

1. **Fluency at coming when called**: The dog should come on one cue (or command) consistently from thirty yards, even in the presence of moderate distraction. A good place to check this out or to train the distraction part is a dog park.
2. **Fluency at delivery to hand**: the dog should consistently deliver to hand.

Deficiencies in these two behaviors usually stem back to punishment that was unknowingly, inadvertently, or accidentally delivered. Neither the how nor the why is relevant. The quickest fix is to give the dog lots of payments (highly desirable treats) for coming to you. If delivery to hand is a weakness, make sure you give the payment when the dog is all the way to you (his nose is within an inch of your leg).

Here is the training model:

1. **Dummies before birds**: Train the dog with dummies. Canvas is better; canvas dummies are comfortable to carry and promote delivery to hand. When the behaviors are well established and fluent with dummies in the face of distraction, you can work the dog on birds and have a low probability of encountering problems. Birds are simply a fairly high distraction level. Save them until the behaviors are fluent in moderate to high distraction levels. Then, working with birds will not create problems.

2. **Blinds before marks:** Blind retrieves are of birds the dog has not seen fall. Marked retrieves are of birds that the dog has seen fall. The dog's ancestor possessed an innate ability to catch and eat a bird he saw land in a distant field. If he did not have this innate talent, then he died. Dogs need very little training on this inherited marking behavior. However, because they trigger such a powerful primary instinct, marks are very disruptive to the training of the gundog's self-control, impulse control, and manners. Marks are like crack cocaine. If the dog has not found out how intoxicating marks are, then whistle stops and hand signals are much more easily trained, and the dog will like these and other control behaviors much more.

3. **Steadiness is primary:** A gundog's primary job is to enhance his owner's outdoor experience. That means he must be obedient, steady, and calm when one hundred ducks are working, duck calls are blaring, and six shooters are shooting. During such periods of extreme excitement, the gundog should be sitting calmly, waiting for instructions. A blind filled with excited hunters and loaded guns is not the place for an overexcited, on-the-edge-of-out-of-control gundog.

The trick here is to let the dog learn from puppyhood that calmness pays (with a retrieve).

The dog should get no marked retrieves without a wait of at least three minutes, as this is the average dissipation time of the neurochemicals that produce the excited emotional state. Sending the dog when he is calm applies the payment of the retrieve to the emotional account of calmness. To further promote calmness and steadiness, pick up most of the seen falls in training yourself or with a second dog.

4. **Long unseen cripple:** This is the gundog's conservation function. Stopping on the whistle and taking directional casts are required for the dog to fetch the birds he has not seen fall. When there are four dead birds down out front of the blind with an unseen, wing-tipped cripple down 125 yards off to the left, the dog needs to get the cripple first, before that bird has a chance to swim off and escape only to die later. This ability is the gundog's most important job.

This behavior is easily trained as a chain ending in a retrieve reward. The chain is of three elements ending with the reward of a dummy. Breaking it down to elements and training them looks like this:

Memory retrieves: the pup goes out without the lure of a fall.

This is the easiest part of the exercise. Simply take the dog with you to place the dummy. He has an innate propensity to go back to the place you left it. After placing the dummy, walk with the dog ten or fifteen yards back whence you came. Send him for the dummy. Then lengthen to thirty yards. He should be going thirty yards with alacrity and confidence within three to five training sessions.

Mark the locations that you are sending the dog from and the location of the dummy for these memory retrieves so that you can accurately use the same setup for a number of upcoming sessions. Then you can progress to whistle stopping.

Stop/Look on whistle.

Note that sitting is not mentioned in the behavior description. Sitting is not necessary for a dog to accomplish blind retrieves. In fact, sitting leads frequently to complicating the exercise. When the whistle blows, the dog stops and looks, and the trainer gets in a fight with the dog about sitting. To the dog, the fight is a punishment for stopping.

Note also that a dog's ears are four times more sensitive than a person's. A dog can hear at one hundred yards a sound that you can barely hear at twenty-five yards. Keep the whistle volume very low when the dog is close to you and out to forty and fifty yards. Then you will accustom him to respond to the volume he will hear when he is three hundred yards from you, when you are blowing loud.

The whistle stop/look is very quick and easy to train, and a tennis ball is an excellent reward with which to pay the dog. To most retrievers, a tennis ball is higher in value than a dummy. Take a tennis ball and make a one-quarter-inch hole through it with a drill. Take a piece of wire eight inches long and bend in middle to a "V" shape. Lay a short length of three-eighths-inch rope across the V. Poke the two ends of the wire through the ball and pull the rope through. Put a knot at each end of the rope so that a six- to eight-inch "tail" extends from the tennis ball. This tail gives you great leverage for longer-distance throws. Practice the throwing to ensure that your motor skills are up to the task of making a well-timed, thirty-yard throw, before you use it with the dog.

Simply take a walk with the pup off leash and encourage him to get ahead of you. When he gets ten to twenty feet away from you, watch his eyes carefully and toot the whistle. When he looks at you, pay the look with a throw. Then go for thirty or forty feet. Your payment throws should soar well past the dog so that they pull him away from you. Your objective is to pay stop/look about five or six times and have the dog responding out to thirty yards. Be careful not to overdo the payments, or you will create a popping (looking to you without a whistle toot) behavior. Too many short payment throws can also contribute to a spinning behavior.

One or two sessions should be enough to have the pup stopping and giving a crisp turn to look at you upon a whistle toot. Then you will have the tools to complete the long unseen cripple exercise. As the pup progresses with the long unseen cripple exercise and continues on to blind retrieves and hunting, you will need to occasionally reinforce the whistle stop with a payment throw. The pup will tell you when it's time by starting to become less consistent in his response to the whistle. Then you need to give him a payment or two. Throw a dummy for shorter-distance stops. Use a tennis ball and racquet or a dummy launcher for longer-distance payments for whistle stops.

Respond to directional cast by leaving area of marked fall and take cast toward the long unseen fall

Here is where you put it all together. Put the place board down for pup's starting point. Then take the pup out thirty yards and place the dummy that serves as the long unseen fall. Then, with the pup, walk back thirty yards to the placeboard. Sit the pup and walk out fifteen yards on an azimuth at least thirty degrees off of the line to the placed unseen. Stop and sequentially throw two dummies with good loft and distance so that the pup is quite interested in them. (If the pup is sitting on a place board back at the starting point, then it is easier for him to stay.) Pick up the two throws. This makes it very difficult for the pup to botch this exercise. Go back to the pup and send him toward the marked falls that have been picked up.

When he gets to the area of fall, give a whistle toot. When the dog looks, walk the direction that you want him to go. You may have to give that whistle toot several times and the walking cue several times to get him to the placed, unseen dummy. It may be pretty ragged the first couple renditions, but that is OK. We are letting the pup learn that he gets paid better when he hunts where you want him to after a whistle stop and cast. It generally takes a few sessions for the pup to get it.

Over a few lessons, you should also fade the walking cue from four or five steps back to one step with a hand signal, and then a half step with a hand signal. The casts are right, left, and back. A back cast should be given with your hand extended straight up high to make it easy for the dog to distinguish from the right and left casts.

That is the basic exercise. Work the pup on it until he is proficient. Then, add distractions. For example, add shots on the thrown marks that you will pick up, add a kid bouncing a basketball, add a guy tossing a dummy for another dog, etc. The key is to add distractions at a low level and gradually increase. For example, start the kid with bouncing basketball at a distance of fifty yards and move him closer gradually, as fast as your dog's performance will allow. Distance is great for damping the level of most distractions.

Start the distraction at a long distance and gradually move it closer at a rate governed by the student dog's success.

When the dog is proficient at a moderate level of distraction, move your initial setup to a different field and do it again. Always remember that the trainer's job is not to test, but to set up the exercise so that the dog will succeed. Thus, the initial run should be set at a simple enough level that you are confident of the pup's success. Then start ratcheting up complexity and distraction level at increments such that the dog continues to succeed. When the pup is proficient in the second location, move again to a third location with initial simplification and building back up the distraction level.

When you have moved the training setup of the long unseen cripple to four or five different locations, the pup should be getting very good. Then you can try him on simple, cold blinds where you have not taken him with you to plant them. When he is good at that, add back the diversion marks. At this point you can probably start leaving the diversion marks lying where they fall and feeling confident that you can handle the pup away from them to fetch the long unseen cripple.

Your goal is to get the dog proficient in a high-distraction environment in four or five different locations. Then the dog should be ready for most situations.

To recap this training model, the objective is to not line the blind. You want a high frequency of occurrence of the behavior chain: go out....., stop/look......., take cast......, get reward (dummy or bird).

Remember that you are simply moving the dog's hunting area from one place to another. You are not trying to produce a robot that engages in precision casting.

Every time the pup lines the blind, he is getting paid to not to stop on a whistle. The higher the frequency of occurrence of lining the blind, the less prone the pup will be to stop on the whistle.

The key to getting whistle-stopping responsiveness at a distance is to crank up the distraction level in the 30-yard zone where you have control of payment delivery. When the pup is fluently stopping at the 30-yard distance in a high-distraction environment, he will stop fluently at 150 yards in a moderate-level-distraction environment.

Try this training model on a young dog that has had few marked retrieves, and you should have him handling well at 150 yards in three to six months of training.

CHAPTER 12

Hunger Games

———◆———

IF YOU WANT TO DEVELOP self-control in your puppy and solidify the behaviors of sitting, staying, casting, and stopping on cue, the hunger game will do it.

Here is a game that gets your puppy trained early. You can start at ten to twelve weeks of age. It is easy and fast to conduct. Use it when feeding your dog. Then training becomes difficult for the trainer to procrastinate. The hunger game is built on two significant behavioral characteristics of dogs. The first factor relates to the dog's ancestors, who had a built-in governor for eating behavior. After the prey was pulled down, the larger wolves ate first, while the underlings waited their turn. To not have such a behavioral model would have meant a lot of fighting over food. The fighting would have expended energy, which must be replenished, and would have resulted in wounds, which would have decreased the recipient's probability of survival. Thus, eating etiquette enhanced higher probability of survival. The hunger game shapes that behavioral propensity of waiting to eat into a more generalized behavior of self-control.

The second factor is that a puppy under six months of age grows at a phenomenally fast rate, which keeps him voraciously hungry most of the time. For a puppy under six months of age, food is usually the highest-value reward and reinforcer of behavior.

When the hunger game is an integral part of the pup's feeding, it is difficult for his master to forget or to procrastinate the training sessions. The basic plan is:

1. Get the pup sitting at the sight of a food bowl held waist high.
2. Get the pup sitting and staying while the food bowl is placed on the ground.
3. Get the pup sitting and staying while the trainer walks thirty feet away, puts down the food bowl, and then returns partway to the pup.
4. Get the pup stopping on the way to the food bowl and then proceeding on cue to the bowl.

Conduct nearly all this training in silence. You want to associate the cue with the desired behavior. After a piece of behavior such as sitting is predictably occurring, add the vocal cue of the word, "Sit." Then the cue is associated with its corresponding behavior— in this case, sitting. Other than pairing the cue with the correct behavior, your voice should be silent. Otherwise, your voice tends to interfere with the training process.

Using a typical twelve-week-old puppy as a student, here is the meal-by-meal lesson plan:

1. When you feed the pup, hold his food bowl high enough that he can't reach it (about waist high). He will dance around and jump around a bit, but finally he will stop and look up at the bowl for some number of seconds. The looking up strains his neck muscles, so after a few more seconds he will sit, at which time you quickly put the bowl on the floor.
2. After five or six meals, he will probably be sitting quickly at the sight of the food bowl. Then you start shaping the sit

for increased duration. To begin, you need to eliminate the race in putting down the bowl to reward him. At the beginning, the pup starts out of the sit at the instant the bowl starts down. When the bowl gets to the ground, the pup is standing, waiting for it. You are probably racing him to get the food down as his rear comes up. You are, in effect, rewarding the pup for standing up. The behavior chain is: sit, s → Stand (quickly), r → Reward (eat).

3. The next step is to eliminate the race with the food bowl. Devote the next couple of sessions to this process.

   When the pup sits, lower the food bowl slowly. When his butt comes off the ground, raise the food bowl. When he sits, again lower the bowl. Start with raising and lowering in increments of a foot or so. Then, as the pup starts responding well, fade the increments down to a few inches.

4. When the pup is responding well by lowering his rear when the food bowl lowers a couple of inches, let him learn that he can make the food go all the way to the floor by remaining sitting. This is a critical step where the dog learns that by offering the behavior of sitting calmly, he can get the food bowl to go down to the ground. He should only get the food when his rear end is touching the ground.

5. When the pup is able to sit calmly until the bowl reaches the ground, start increasing the time interval of sitting while the bowl is down. Start with a one-half-second delay before releasing him with a hand gesture to go from the sit to the bowl. You may need to use a slight "hiss" with a raised-hand, "traffic cop" gesture to help him stay at first. Over the next five sessions, increase his wait time to ten seconds. If he fails, shorten up the wait interval for a couple of sessions, and then proceed.

6. When he is proficient at sitting calmly for ten seconds before being released to eat, you can start increasing the

distance from the pup to the bowl. Start with the bowl at three feet from the pup with a wait of two seconds, then go to three seconds, then to four feet. Then gradually progress to thirty or forty feet. The release gesture should be a hand signal and step in the appropriate direction.

7. The pup will quickly become proficient at the forty-foot cast to the food bowl. Achieve proficiency on both left- and right-hand casts. Then you can progress to a stop on cue.

8. Next, add on the stop whistle. Sit the pup, walk forty feet from him, and put down the food bowl. This works better if the forty-foot travel path is along a wall or fence. Then walk halfway back to the pup and move two steps off his travel path. Cast him toward the food and, when he has traveled six feet, give a soft whistle toot and step toward travel path with a raised hand. When he stops, pause a second, and then step back while giving the cast gesture toward the food bowl. After several sessions of stopping, you can fade the step (while keeping the soft whistle toot) and start standing farther away from the pup's travel path. Your goal is to move yourself gradually to a point such that the pup is casting away from you toward the food bowl, and you are stopping him on the way to the bowl and then casting him onward to it.

Points to watch are:

1. "Program" equal amounts of left casts, right casts, and back casts, so that the pup has equal propensity for each cast.

2. Keep the stop whistle soft. A dog's ears are four times more sensitive than a human's. If you program the pup to stop on a loud whistle blast at forty feet, then there will be insufficient volume at one hundred yards to trigger a response.

When the pup is proficient with the casting and stopping, start introducing distraction in the area where the pup operates with confidence. Some examples would be:

1. Put a kid twenty feet away, bouncing a basketball, while the pup is performing his casting and stopping.
2. Then add a second kid and have both make noise while bouncing basketballs.
3. Have someone walk a dog around the yard while the pup is performing his task. Then bring the other dog closer.
4. Have a couple of kids make noise and toss a football while the pup is performing. Start with the kids at twenty yards' distance. At the next session, bring them to ten yards. At the third session, bring them to a ten-foot distance from the pup's training area.
5. Borrow a couple of chickens or ducks and let them wander around while the pup is performing.
   Use distance to initially attenuate the distraction level.

The early exposure to distraction will serve the pup well in the future when you ask him to perform in new and strange environments.

When the pup is proficient at casting and stopping with food bowls in the yard and with distraction, he will have an excellent foundation for future fieldwork on blind retrieves.

CHAPTER 13

Frequency and Duration
of Training Sessions

———

WHEN I STARTED TRAINING RETRIEVERS as a professional in 1972, I thought that the dogs needed to be trained six days a week for at least a half hour each. After the first several hundred dogs, I began to notice that some weeks, when I skipped a day or two of training, a lot of dogs seemed to make great strides in training. Over the years, I have found by trial and error that dogs seem to train much faster on a schedule of training every other day. I further found that most of the times that a dog has had a light-bulb moment and mastered a difficult behavior in an astonishingly fast rate, it has usually been a dog that hasn't been worked for a week or two for various reasons. I have found that one can produce some great leaps forward in a dog's training program by leaving him in the kennel for a week or two, and then training a really difficult behavior.

I have also found that keeping lessons very short and focused on one learning objective leads to the fastest overall training. If I ignore the travel time walking at heel to get to the training area, the core piece of the training lesson lasts typically three to five minutes. That time length is optimum for learning in dogs. Two obvious exceptions on brevity of sessions are training on honoring and steadiness and when performing long water retrieves.

In the last few years, research has been done which bolsters my viewpoint.

In 2010, a project analyzing frequency and duration of canine training sessions was conducted at the University of Copenhagen. This recent study involved forty-four dogs divided into four groups. The groups were:

1. W1—trained weekly at one session per day, one day per week.
2. W3—trained weekly at three sessions per day, one day per week.
3. D1—trained daily at one session per day, five days per week.
4. D3—trained daily at three sessions per day, five days per week.

Here is the abstract:

Abstract

Most domestic dogs are subjected to some kind of obedience training, often on a frequent basis, but the question of how often and for how long a dog should be trained has not been fully investigated. Optimizing the training as much as possible is not only an advantage in the training of working dogs such as guide dogs and police dogs, but also the training of family dogs can benefit from this knowledge. We studied the effect of frequency and duration of training sessions on acquisition and on long-term memory. Forty-four laboratory beagles were divided into four groups and trained by means of operant conditioning and shaping to perform a traditional obedience task, each dog having a total of eighteen training sessions. The training schedules of the four groups differentiated in frequency (one to two times per week vs. daily) and duration (one training session vs. three training sessions in a row). Acquisition was measured as achieved training level at a certain time. The dogs' retention of the task was tested four weeks postacquisition. Results demonstrated that dogs trained one to two times per week had significantly better acquisition than daily trained dogs, and that dogs trained only one session a day had significantly better acquisition than dogs trained three sessions in a row. The interaction between frequency and duration of training sessions was also significant, suggesting that the two affect acquisition differently depending on the combination of these. The combination of weekly training and one session resulted in the highest level of acquisition, whereas the combination of daily training and three sessions in a row resulted in the lowest level of acquisition. Daily training in one session produced similar results as weekly training combined with three sessions in a row. Training schedule did not affect retention of the learned task; all groups had a high level of retention after four weeks. The results of the study can be used to optimize training in dogs, which is important since the number of training sessions often is a limiting factor in practical dog training. The results also suggest that, once a task is learned, it is likely to be remembered for a period of at least four weeks after last practice, regardless of frequency and duration of the training sessions.

(Helle, Demanta, Jan Ladewigb, Thorsten J. S. Balsbya, Torben Dabelsteena. "The Effect of Frequency and Duration of Training Sessions on Acquisition and Long-Term Memory in Dogs." Abstract. University of Copenhagen, Faculty of Science, Department of Biology. Universitetsparken 15, DK-2100 København Ø Denmark. University of Copenhagen, Faculty of Life Sciences, Department of Large Animal

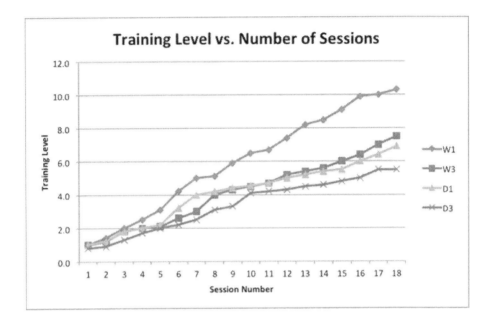

Sciences. Grønnegårdsvej 8, DK-1870, Frederiksberg C, Denmark)

Looking at the graph of learning curves for the four groups, one can generalize:

1. The dogs that trained one session per week (W1) learned the fastest.
2. The dogs that trained three sessions per day, five days per week (D3) showed the slowest rate of learning.
3. The learning level achieved in eighteen sessions was nearly twice as high in the W1 dogs compared to the D3 dogs. Looking at the slope of the curves, it also appears that the D3 dogs will never catch up with the W1 dogs.

A pertinent fact in this study is that the all the dogs were in a controlled environment. When not in a training session, they were confined to pens. A typical family dog/gundog will probably be living in the house, playing with the kids, etc. That is great. It develops the dog's communication skills and gives great enjoyment to the family. However, some structure should be imposed upon the dog's activities and behaviors, especially those that compete with behaviors being trained.

The prime example of a critical behavior and an unstructured environment during nontraining time is steadiness. If you are giving the dog ten reinforcements per session or twenty reinforcements per session for sitting quietly while training dummies are thrown, and, unknown to you, the kids are giving the dog thirty or forty reinforcements a day for breaking for a tennis ball throw, then the breaking behavior is going to predominate. Some control must be maintained over the dog's environment. The dog must be prevented from learning behaviors that are in conflict with a trained gundog. The desired behaviors are obedience, coming when called, and steadiness for fallen objects. Thus, games of chase and uncontrolled retrieves should not be played. Then your gundog-training program can be effective, whether it is conducted one day per week or five days a week. The Copenhagen study says that the dog will be trained faster and to a higher level on the one-day-per-week schedule.

This study demonstrated that less training is better. The schedule I recommend is every other day. This suggestion should be great news for those that think they don't have enough time to train a gundog.

CHAPTER 14

The Trainer's Behavior

1. Train from the perspective that the dog wants to do what you want, and that the major obstacle is you communicating what you want.

2. Keep your mouth shut. Your voice is distracting to the dog and simply makes it more difficult for the dog to do what you want. Save the talking until the desired behavior is fluent, and then use talking as part of your program to develop fluency of the behavior in the presence of distraction.

3. Try to maintain some body movement on the part of the trainer, so that the dog is getting some additional information. Remember that the dog's primary communication is visual, in the form of seeing your body language. The trainer's movements should be calm and methodical as opposed to fast and jerky.

4. Whenever the dog is having trouble mastering a behavior, the solution lies in simplifying the behavior or lowering the distraction level. Frequently, the distraction level can be lowered by moving farther away from the distraction.

5. The trainer should remember this principle:
   If the dog is not performing the behavior that you want, then one or all of these axioms are being violated:
   - The trainer is asking for a behavior for which he has not adequately trained.

or

- The trainer is asking the dog to perform a behavior in presence of a distraction level for which the trainer has not prepared the dog.

6. The trainer should develop the necessary motor skills to succeed at training. When you are rewarding with treats, you will be the most successful if your motor skills are good. You should be able to deliver up to thirty treats per minute without spilling them on the ground. The treat should also be offered from your open palm, as some dogs will make a game out of nipping at your fingers when you are delivering a treat held with fingertips.

   When rewarding with a retrieve, you need to be able to throw far enough and accurately enough to ensure the dog's success. You should be able to reliably throw a dummy twenty to thirty yards and have it land within a six-foot circle. For most folks, this motor skill requires a little practice to achieve.

CHAPTER 15

Hunting Your Dog: Upland Dog, Shed Dog, Deer Dog

———◆———

AFTER YOU HAVE PUT ALL the effort into training your dog, there are a few suggestions that will make it easier for you to maintain that state. First and foremost, make sure he enjoys his first few hunts. Remember to introduce the pup to the gun and ensure that he is comfortable with shooting before he goes hunting.

INTRODUCTION TO THE GUN

It is important to introduce the dog to the gun well before taking him hunting. The easiest method I have found involves the dog watching another dog retrieve in the water, initially from a distance and gradually moved closer. The dog determines how fast you move toward the gun. When you arrive at the gun, give the trainee a retrieve or two with a shot. You are associating the dog's highest-value activity with the sound of the gun. With most dogs, it only takes about ten or fifteen minutes.

Use a shotgun. Dogs appear to be less prone to anxiety with the frequency signature of a shotgun. The higher frequency of a .22 seems to be more irritating to some dogs.

First Hunts

On the pup's first hunts, take a leash. Keep him under control. He needs to learn early that hunting is a place to be under control. Place him ten or fifteen yards from the gun. On the first few hunts, the pup probably doesn't know where the birds are coming from. In order to learn that, he needs to see one flying along get shot and fall. After seeing one or two occurrences of birds being hit and falling, the light bulb will come on.

Typically, a dog on his first hunt will look at the gun each time it shoots. Automatics and pumps that are kicking out empty cartridges reinforce that behavior. Looking at the gun at every shot makes it difficult for the pup to see a flying bird get hit, unless the pup is sitting ten or fifteen yards from the gun. Then, when the pup looks at the gun, he will see plenty of peripheral sky and will readily see the bird falls that he needs for his education.

Age and First Hunts

Age is not the issue. The issues are proficiency of behaviors and physical maturity. The pup needs to be fairly proficient at coming when called and delivering to hand. He needs to have been introduced to gunshots. He also should have had a chance to retrieve a bird or two prior to hunting. If he is not steady and obedient, then keep him on a leash except during retrieves.

He also needs to be comfortable. The owner needs to keep him from being too hot or too cold. It is not a good idea to hunt a dog under eighteen months of age in extremely cold water. Under that age, his muscle mass is likely not sufficient to keep him warm enough on long swims.

HEARING PROTECTION

Don't forget that the pup's ears are four times more sensitive than a human's ears. That also means they are four times more delicate and easy to damage with too many decibels. Put the pup where the noise levels from shooting will be lowest. That would be eight or ten feet behind you, away from the direction in which you will be shooting.

When you hunt in a sunken-pit blind, do not put the dog in the bottom of the blind. Put him outside the pit. The noise levels produced by several guys shooting three-inch magnums from a pit blind is tremendous in the bottom of the pit.

STEADINESS: WAIT THREE MINUTES ON DEAD BIRDS

It is not uncommon for a fairly well-trained young dog to come unglued and lose his steadiness during his first season of hunting. It goes to brain chemistry and sloppy human habits. Mother Nature has endowed predators like the dog with some specialized brain chemistry to enhance survival. When your retriever sees a bird flying, he gets a small jolt of adrenaline, dopamine, and endorphins that get him ready to go after prey. When the dog initiates the physical activity of chasing that prey, he gets another, larger dose of neurochemicals to enable him to run faster. When the dog gets to the bird, he gets another jolt of brain chemicals to enable him to kill it (in case the prey is large). All these neurotransmitters constitute a huge reward to the dog. If, when you release the dog to retrieve, he is in an elevated emotional state, then you are rewarding that emotional state.

It takes about three minutes for those neurotransmitters to dissipate and allow the dog to return to a calm state. When you release the calm dog to retrieve, you are rewarding the emotional state of calmness.

Many times with different dogs, I have thrown a bird out in the pond for a retrieve. I don't release them for the retrieve until they are emotionally calm. My measuring device to determine the dog's state of excitement is a treat. When I offer a treat and the dog is not interested, I know he is still in a state of excitement. When I offer a treat, and he takes it, he is calm. Then, I release him to retrieve. The time period from the splash of the fall to the calmness of the dog typically will be three minutes. Over a number of retrieves, the dog's period of excitement will shorten as he learns and accepts the waiting period.

You can think of this as two bank accounts: the wildness account and the calmness account. Send the dog quickly on a shot bird, and you are paying the wildness account. Wait three minutes to send the dog on a shot bird, and you are paying the calmness account.

If you want your dog to remain calm and steady during hunting, then wait at least three minutes before sending him for dead birds.

PICK CRIPPLED BIRDS FIRST

Dogs are fairly easy to manipulate into making choices if the trainer is good at using relative values of rewards. If you want the dog to make the decision to retrieve cripples first, just increase the value of the cripple. This technique is fairly easy to do with duck hunting. If you make the dog wait at least three minutes before retrieving a dead bird and send him at three seconds on a cripple, then the cripple is going to have a much higher value to the dog. He will begin preferring the cripples.

As an added benefit, the dog's superior motion detection will enable the dog to identify a cripple in the first ten to twenty feet of fall. Fairly quickly, he will quit watching dead birds all the way down in order to look around at the next shot to see if a cripple is going to fall.

Dogs typically fail to see a bird shot because they are busily looking at a dead bird on the water in anticipation of being sent immediately. When you lower the value of the dead bird with the three-minute wait, the dog readily turns to the next shot, looking for a cripple to fall. You will end up with very few unseen falls of cripples and drastically reduce the number of lost cripples.

EXTREMELY HOT WEATHER

From the standpoint of evolution, dogs have survived extreme weather quite well over thousands of years. However, the last two hundred years have brought a change in breeding selection. Man has replaced Mother Nature in the breeding selection process. Increasingly, we have been selectively breeding retrievers to build their drive. One effect of this selective breeding has been the decrease or elimination of the "off switch" in many retrievers. Today, many retrievers will keep going even though it may kill them. It is the responsibility of today's retriever owner to learn how to act as a governor on some of the dog's activities, in order to keep him safe. To the dog, the most dangerous environment is heat.

Every dove season in the South, a number of dogs die from heatstroke. Those deaths are easy to prevent. Hunters traditionally get wrapped up in learning and recognizing the symptoms of heat exhaustion and trying to manage the problem after the symptoms appear. That is a high-risk strategy. If you wait until the symptoms appear, the dog probably has about a 50 percent probability of dying. Manage the heat, and keep the symptoms from appearing. That is the safest strategy for your dog. Basically, it boils down to rationing his strenuous exercise and keeping him wet or damp on the outside when he is working in high-temperature conditions. Since muscle movement is the producer of heat in a dog, managing heat levels means managing exercise levels.

A dog's normal body temperature is 101–102.5 degrees Fahrenheit. Strenuous exercise will spike that body temperature up to the range of 106–108 degrees. The dog's body cannot withstand that high a temperature for extended periods. He will go into irreversible heatstroke and die. He has to lose some of that body heat fairly quickly. If it is 95 degrees, and you have three doves downed in a soybean field, and the dog has just hunted vigorously for five minutes before returning with the first one, don't immediately send him for number two. Sit him down in the shade for ten or fifteen minutes and let him lose some heat. Then, send him for the next downed bird. Moderating his activity levels will keep his body heat at manageable levels.

Your second major tool for helping your dog fight heat is evaporation. Evaporation literally sucks heat out of the air in the vicinity of a wet surface. That is why you feel cool when you walk into a forest. As part of their metabolic cycle, trees evaporate water off of their leaves. A single tree evaporates hundreds of gallons of water per day. A building benefitting from the active evaporative cooling of trees will experience a 17 percent reduction in cooling requirement. Just think of the benefit of a 17 percent reduction in heat to a dog on a hot day.

When water evaporates it goes from the liquid to the gaseous state. The process absorbs energy in the form of heat. When you step out of the shower and feel chilled, that is evaporation working. Evaporation can lower the temperature in the immediate surrounding area five to ten degrees. Evaporation is also proportionate to the surface area that is wet. Unlike people, dogs do not sweat. With a dry dog, evaporation is limited mainly to the surface area of the mucous membranes of his nose, mouth, and throat. With a dog that is wet over his entire body, the surface area of evaporation is increased hugely, and the dog will much more readily lose heat.

When you are hunting in hot weather, a good practice is to start with the dog wet and to keep him damp if possible. That way, you start with him cool and help him to stay cool from evaporation.

Several cautions are in order for wet dogs and heat.

1. Don't put a wet dog in an enclosed space like a dog crate. The lack of air circulation will severely curtail evaporation and allow heat to build up.
2. Before counting on a small pond to cool your dog, stick your finger in the water. If it feels warm, then immersion is not going to cool the dog. Put him in for a moment to wet him down, and then bring him out for evaporative cooling to go to work.

Manage your dog's heat levels long before he gets too hot. That is the best protection against heatstroke.

EXTREMELY COLD WEATHER

Cold water can kill your dog also. Cold water acts as a heat sink and sucks the body heat off of the dog. The length of time the dog is in the water is the critical factor. The longer the immersion, the more heat the dog loses. A major management tool is, again, moderating his activity. If you have knocked down three ducks, and the dog just spent five minutes swimming in cold water to collect the first one, get him out of the water and let him build back body heat for ten or fifteen minutes before sending him for the next bird.

Keep him out of the water when he is not retrieving. Even if the pup is standing in shallow water, the water still robs him of body heat—just at a lower rate. Put him on a stand, a log, or in the boat—some place where he is completely removed from the water. Get him a neoprene vest. The vest will help him retain body heat. Also, try to place him where the wind is blocked. Wind removes body heat also.

Don't give your dog a bath during waterfowl season. Soap and detergent wash the oils out of his coat and rob him of his natural waterproofing. That means he loses a lot of body heat when his insulating undercoat gets wet.

Lastly and most importantly, watch out for ice. One of the most dangerous situations for the dog arises when he is hunting on ice and breaks through. He may not be able to climb out. If you have ever watched or helped a dog climb into a boat, you have seen that he needs to get purchase on some surface with his back feet to propel himself up into the boat. We usually offer a substitute in the form of a hand on the back of his neck, which allows his front legs to gain the additional leverage necessary to pull himself up into the boat. When he falls through thin ice, he may not have the hind leg purchase to pull himself back up on the ice. This is where his dewclaws can be a lifesaver. A dog that has fallen through the ice will instinctively stretch out his front legs and rotate them inward to hook the dewclaws into the ice. If the dewclaws are present, then he has a much greater probability of pulling himself out and up onto the ice.

Whenever you hunt on ice, it is good to have a plan B. If the dog falls through the ice and can't get out, you are going to have a problem that requires some equipment such as a small boat to slide across the ice to get you safely to the dog for rescue.

A little attention spent on heat management in extreme temperature settings, either hot or cold, will go long way in helping your dog deal with a hostile environment.

UPLAND HUNTING

For upland hunting, the quarry will typically be pheasants, and the behaviors required will be quartering and sit-to-flush. The dog's job will be quartering closely enough to the hunter so that the birds flushed will be close enough to kill.

Quartering is an easy-to-produce behavior. Basically, it is based on keeping the dog close enough that the birds he flushes will be within range by the time you get your gun up and your finger on the trigger. Typically, the bird that flushes at fifteen yards will be at about thirty yards when you have the gun up and are ready to shoot.

The pup needs to quarter at fifteen yards. To accomplish this feat, simply make sure his recall is very fluent in a high-distraction environment and then take him hunting in an area with plenty of pheasant scent. As you walk along, consistently call the pup back whenever he passes the fifteen-yard limit. Soon he will confine himself to the fifteen yards and hunt to the left or right instead of away from you. When you need to communicate a directional change, simply make a noise to attract his attention and take a few steps in the desired direction to prompt him to change his direction.

Have you seen that photo of flushing pheasant about ten feet off the ground with a Labrador's reaching mouth just beneath his tail feathers? That is a very dangerous position for the dog to be in. Several dogs are killed every year in pheasant country by hunters with overanxious trigger fingers. An ounce of prevention pays here.

Train the dog to sit-to-flush. To accomplish this behavior, the prerequisite is good impulse control, which the dog mastered in his basic duckdog training. To add sit-to-flush to his behaviors, he needs only to learn to sit from a walk and then to sit from a walk during a high-distraction moment. Here is how to do it:

1. Put a leash on the pup and walk along with him at heel (he should already be quite proficient at heeling and sitting).
2. Toss a dummy eight or ten feet out front (a short dinky toss is a lower distraction level, making it easier for him to sit). The dummy tossed to the front is the "flushing bird" and is not retrieved. As the dummy leaves your hand, stop walking and say, "Sit." After the pup sits, toss a dummy over your shoulder to land six feet behind you. Let the pup continue

sitting for a few seconds, and then let him retrieve the short "behind you" dummy. After he retrieves the short dummy, leave him sitting and walk out and pick up the "flushing" dummy yourself.

3. This short, "behind you" dummy is the pup's reward for sitting for the forward "flushing" dummy. Over the next few repetitions of this exercise, the forward "flushing" dummy throw will become much higher and farther, and the sit-and-wait interval will become longer. The short, reward dummy tossed behind you will remain short and be put on a variable schedule.

4. Over several sessions, raise the distraction level of the "flushing" dummy by adding gunshots, other dogs, a dummy launcher, etc. When the pup is solid on dummies, run the exercise with dead birds, and then clip wing pigeons. Never let him retrieve the flushing bird out front. For the sit-to-flush, pay the pup occasionally with the short toss behind you of a dummy or tennis ball.

Train the sit-to-flush behavior before you go hunting, and you can train the quartering behavior as you hunt.

Shed Dog

Collecting shed deer antlers is becoming a popular pastime. Your duck retriever can be easily taught to help you in this endeavor. The first principle for shed training is that the dog naturally likes shed antlers. Most dogs when given a shed antler, will use it as a chew toy. For training, you simply increase the value of a shed toy by allowing the dog to retrieve it. Then let him discover that bringing an antler chew to you will get you to throw it for him to retrieve. Here is a training plan:

1. Google "shed deer antler chews for dogs."
2. Order some deer antler chew toys.
3. Let the dog chew a bit on an antler section.
4. Give him a few retrieves of the antler chew.
5. Take him out and give him a few retrieves of the antler chew in a patch of cover.
6. Go back the next day and, unseen by the dog, place a few antler chews in the same patch of cover that he retrieved from the day before.
7. Bring the dog and encourage him to find the antler chews.
8. When he gets an antler chew, encourage him to bring it to you.
9. When he arrives, take it and give him a retrieve of the chew.

A few sessions of the dog hunting up chews and getting a retrieve reward will have him ready to go shed hunting with you. All you have to do is maintain a variable schedule of reinforcement of his shed-hunting behavior by occasionally tossing a just-found shed for him to retrieve.

BLOOD-TRAILING DEER DOG

If you are a bow hunter and want a dog who will trail a wounded deer, then your training task is the easiest. A dog is a natural tracker of game. It is a behavior he is born with. Simply train him as a duckdog and then give him enough hunting experience to include the opportunity of tracking down a dozen or more wounded ducks. Tracking down a like number of wounded pheasants will further enhance the dog's tracking talent. These tracking opportunities should develop his inherent tracking propensity sufficiently that it will generalize to a deer-blood trail. When you put him on a deer-blood trail, your major difficulty will be keeping up with the dog as he follows the trail. Putting a leash on him may interfere with his tracking to the extent that he stops. Therefore, let him do his deer tracking off leash. This may require a little jogging on your part to keep up with the dog.

The key to easy and successful training is to recognize and reinforce the dog's natural, inherited behaviors, while accentuating and reinforcing his self-control and without inhibiting his hunting initiative.

CHAPTER 16

Housetraining and Heeling

———

Two dog behaviors that people seem to have a lot of trouble training are housebreaking and heeling.

Both behaviors are fairly easy to train if approached from the proper perspective.

Housetraining

The principles of evolution say that puppies have a natural proclivity to eliminate outside the den. If they did not, then the probability of disease would be high. Eliminating outside the den carries with it a survival value. Thus, the dog has an innate propensity not to foul his own nest. All the human needs to do is make it easy for the dog to exercise that innate behavior. It is essentially a matter of schedule management. Here is how to accomplish this task:

1. Get the dog a crate to be his "den." The crate should be of a size that he can comfortably turn around and lie down. It should not be much larger. Keep him in the crate when he is unsupervised. The basic principle is to adjust his environment so that he only eliminates when he is outside. This trains the behavior of eliminating outdoors. The act of eliminating is a reward in itself. If you take him to a particular area in the yard every time and give him a treat, he will

form a preference for eliminating in that place. Whenever you want to let him out of the crate for indoor activity, always take him from the crate directly outdoors and let him eliminate before turning him loose in the house.

2. Established a fixed schedule. Feed the dog the same time or times each day. Let him outside on a fixed schedule. The only way a dog can predict what time to expect dinner is by what the schedule was yesterday, and the day before, and the day before. The same principle applies to going outside.

   An adult dog's digestive time for canned dog food averages about four to six hours to move through his system. With dry food, it may take as long as eight to ten hours. A puppy's cycle time will be much faster. Stress and many other factors will also alter cycle time. In other words, it is quite difficult to pin down. It is best to err to the conservative side. My rule of thumb is two hours for young puppies and four hours for adults.

3. Limit the intake. If you cut back 50 percent on the dog's food for the first three days of housebreaking, you make it easy for him to "hold it," and thus easier for him to adjust his schedule to your fixed (and thus predictable) schedule.

4. The best regimen for night confinement for puppies is:
   • Give evening meal at 4:00 p.m. in the afternoon.
   • No water after 6:00 p.m. in the evening.
   • Take out at 11:00 p.m. and then put in the crate.
   • Wake up at 5:00 a.m. and take outside.
   Most puppies over ten weeks of age can adapt readily to this schedule if the schedule is regular and the puppy is on a sparse serving size of food.

5. Major contributors to difficulty with housebreaking are:
   • Irregular schedule imposed by the human
   • Overfeeding
   • Unsupervised puppy activities in the house

If you follow the above principles, you should be able to housetrain a puppy or dog in three to five days.

HEELING

Whenever I discuss heeling, I have to throw in a horse story that relates. Back in the seventies, I was going to an occasional Ray Hunt horse-training clinic. Ray was the original horse whisperer. He was an absolutely superb practitioner of positive training with horses. I took a horse that had a loading problem to one of Ray's clinics. She wouldn't walk into a trailer without an argument.

At the clinic, I was standing behind my stock trailer, holding the mare by her halter rope, and I asked Ray, "Would you help get this mare to load into the trailer without a fight?"

"Sure," said Ray. "Just take the lead rope lightly and lead the horse in without pulling."

"OK," I said, and proceeded, lead rope in hand, into the trailer. The mare jerked me right back out.

Ray walked over and said, "Hold your hand up and stick out your trigger finger."

I did that, and Ray hung the lead rope over my extended finger. "Walk in the trailer," he said.

I walked into the trailer, and the mare followed me right in. The moral of the story is that a horse has an opposition reflex, and so does a human when he grasps a rope in the palm of his hand. The horse had a different definition than I did for pulling on a rope.

The same situation arises in getting a dog to heel when he is wearing a collar and lead. The trainer pulls a little, and the dog pulls back a little, and pretty soon the dog is pulling the trainer down the street like a sled dog pulling a sled. In order to stop, one of them has to quit pulling. If the human simply drops his end of the lead on the ground and simply walks along and treats when the dog is in the correct position, heeling will ensue fairly quickly.

A new trainer will have a much greater probability of success at training the dog to heel if he trains him initially off leash. Start where you don't have to worry about the dog leaving. That might be in a small, fenced backyard, or a gymnasium, or any large, empty room or space bounded with a wall or fence. When you have a good place to start, simply take the dog and begin walking. Every time he arrives at the heel position, reach down and give him a treat without interrupting your walking.

Very quickly the dog will be walking at heel for ten to twenty feet of travel. Gradually and rapidly increase that distance. Then, bring in some distractions to strengthen the behavior. When the behavior is fairly fluent, add the leash back into the scenario.

Most novice trainers are very poor at training the behavior of heeling with the leash on the dog and in the trainer's hand. If you find yourself walking along, holding the lead and jerking on the dog's neck while the dog is within two or three feet, you are, in effect, punishing the dog for being close to you. Those punishments are going to interfere with the dog's behavior of coming to you, and those punishments will affect other areas of behavior such as delivery to hand.

The solution is to drop your end of the lead and start paying the dog when he is in the proper heel position.

CHAPTER 17

A History of Labradors and Field Trials

———◆———

HISTORY OF LABRADORS

THE LABRADOR RETRIEVER ORIGINATED IN the English fishing fleets of the sixteenth and seventeenth centuries. During that era, cod was a highly sought commodity. Codfish dried well and were easily preserved by treatment with salt. Cod was thus a valued food to sustain armies and navies. A large number of meatless religious days for predominantly Catholic populations also drove up demand for fish. At the end of the fifteenth century, more Europeans were engaged in fishing than in any other occupation except farming.

The English began fishing the banks off Newfoundland in the fifteenth century. By 1615, the English fishing vessels working the banks off Newfoundland numbered around 250. The typical English fishing vessels carried a number of small dories, which were offloaded and from which the fishermen caught cod on hand lines. The single hand line carried two hooks at its end, allowing the fisherman to haul up two cod at a time. At the depths fished, it might take a fisherman a half hour to bring in a fish or a pair of fish. As the fish were brought from the water into the boat, there was a great opportunity for a fish to flop off of the primitive fishhook. That freed fish would be in a comatose state for a few seconds, and an alert dog would have a chance to hop in the water and fetch him into the boat. Such a dog would have had a significant economic value.

In the fifteenth and sixteenth centuries, very few people had enough to eat. Farming was primitive. There was no refrigeration. To feed a dog often meant taking food from your children. A dog had to have great value in those times to survive being eaten as emergency rations during times of food scarcity. The fishing dog that became the Labrador was a dog of significant value. That fish-catching, ancestral Labrador would have been the last dog to be eaten as emergency rations during a time of famine.

The early fishing fleets also left behind some work crews to maintain the shore infrastructure and the drying racks and to cut wood over the winter. Settlements came and went. Working dogs became an integral part of the fishing activities in summer. These same dogs served in winter as hunting dogs to help the settlers gather in the game that served to supplement the humans' diet. One would expect that the major economic role played by these dogs would fairly ruthlessly drive a breeding selection process for a hardworking, efficient retriever with great talent in cold water. Over the course of several hundred years, these dogs would become the ancestors of the St. John's Water Dog of the island of Newfoundland.

In the seventeen hundreds and eighteen hundreds, the advent of the flintlock, followed by percussion fowling pieces in Europe, ushered in the age of sporting guns and the shooting of birds for sport, an activity that was enthusiastically embraced by the gentry of England. As the sport of shooting fowl became popular, so did the endeavor of using dogs to find and fetch the harvest. In the late seventeen hundreds and early eighteen hundreds, the English sportsmen began developing several breeds of dogs to find, point, and fetch the quarry. One of these breeds was the Labrador, which was bred originally from the St. John's Water Dog.

The main two early breeders of the Labrador were the 5th Duke of Buccleuch in Scotland and the 2nd Earl of Malmesbury in southern England. The Duke of Buccleuch bred them for their excellence as gundogs to serve his gamekeepers for his estates in Scotland. The Earl of Malmesbury bred them for use in duck shooting on his estate at Heron Court on the south coast of Dorset, because of the Labrador's acknowledged expertise in waterfowling.

The two breeding programs flourished independently until the early 1880s when the 6th Duke of Buccleuch and the 3rd Earl of Malmesbury met by chance while shooting. The Earl of Malmesbury subsequently gave to Buccleuch some of his impressive waterfowling Labradors.

The 6th Duke of Buccleuch mated bitches of the original strain to the Malmesbury waterfowling strain and produced the impressive Labradors that were the foundation of today's talented Labrador breed. Beginning with Buccleuch Ned in 1882 and Buccleuch Avon in 1885, a strong bloodline was developed—a bloodline that figured prominently in winners of early British field trials.

Shortly after the death of the 3rd Earl of Malmesbury in 1889, the Malmesbury kennel ceased operating, leaving the Labrador to be preserved by the dukes of Buccleuch. The Buccleuch Kennels are unique in that the original strain of Labrador imported in the 1830s has been strictly maintained to the present day.

BRITISH SHOOTING

With the advent of breech-loading guns and cartridges in the mid-1800s, the sport of shooting flying birds began to arise in England. Queen Victoria's son, Edward, Prince of Wales, took up shooting. He bought the twenty-thousand-acre estate Sandringham in 1864 and began developing it for shooting. Edward's passion for shooting, along with the increase in rail systems in England, led to the evolution of the Victorian Shooting Party. These events were affairs of several days, held on country estates with large shoots in the daytime and elaborate dinners and balls at night. The bag of the shoots was a matter of some competition, with larger shoots achieving bags up in the thousands of birds, mainly pheasants.

By the early nineteen hundreds, these driven shoots had become well structured. They functioned along the same lines as the United Kingdom driven shooting of today. The planning begins a year or more in advance of the shooting season with the planting of the plots of small grains that will feed the pheasants during the coming summer and fall. During the summer, six-week-old pheasants are released into a "release pen" consisting of several acres enclosed by a fence of wire netting of a size to contain the young birds and exclude ground predators. There is no top to the pen.

When the young birds are first released into the pen, the outer feathers of one wing are clipped to restrict flight for the two weeks necessary for the feathers to grow back. The birds are fed well in the release pen, and it becomes a sanctuary to them.

After two weeks in the release pen, some of the birds will start flying over the perimeter fence. When the young pheasants try to reenter the pen, they tend to run on the ground. Many will try to get back in by poking along the bottom of the wire fence. The way back will be "pop" holes, which will have been opened as soon as the birds started flying over the boundary fence.

The pop holes are small, ground-level entrance holes in the wire with a one-way funnel attached to make it easy for the birds to come back in but difficult for them to exit. The pop holes are large enough to admit a small pheasant but exclude foxes and similar-sized ground predators. Additionally, there will be a hot wire extending around the perimeter at top and bottom to further exclude ground predators. As the pheasants mature and start moving in and out of the release pen more freely, more of them will learn to fly back in. The reluctant flyers will be herded back into the release pen with dogs in a practice called dogging in. This accelerates the birds proficiency at flying back into the release pen. Over time, the birds get wilder and spend more time out and about the farm. If the right feed crops and coverts are planted, the birds will spend their days out feeding and loafing, returning in the evenings to the release pen to roost. By the time the shooting season opens, they are fairly wild.

The gamekeeper plans, structures, and plants the drives over many years. Planting the feed plots for the pheasants is the easiest part. Using the basic principle that the flushed birds will head for their release pen, he plants copses of woods for cover and strategically plants rows of trees to push the flushing birds up in altitude. If he has a deep valley, he will use it to gain altitude on the birds' flight path. The goal of the gamekeeper is to produce birds at high speed and altitude that will be a challenge for the guns. This is accomplished by using terrain and trees. The shoot has a number of players involved. The guns are the critical players. They pay the bills. Typically, there will be eight to ten guns who are paying for the day of shooting. Typically, they will be paying £30 to £35 per bird. The day's bag is agreed to beforehand, and the driving and flushing will be geared to the shooting of that number of birds. The gamekeeper who orchestrates this production will, in the first drive or two, get a good idea of the skill level of the guns and will adjust the selection of subsequent drives and the beating and flushing rates to produce, by the end of the day, the agreed bag number. Generally, they will end up within 5 percent of the target number. The typical bag in Victorian days sometimes ran in the thousands. Today, the typical bag is in the range of one hundred to three hundred birds for eight to ten guns.

The other major players in this production are the beaters, the pickers-up, and the dogs. A typical shoot, depending on size, will have twelve to thirty beaters. Many of them will have dogs with them to help with the flushing. The beaters' role is to gently move the birds from feeding areas to concentrate them in cover and then to flush them in an organized manner from that cover. The dogs are essential to the flushing. Equally essential is the dogs being under control so that the process can be somewhat controlled. Beaters with controlled dogs are highly valued and necessary. Out-of-control dogs are not tolerated.

The remaining essential players to the shoot are the pickers-up. Usually there will be one picker-up per gun. Typically, the picker-up will have two or three dogs. Sometimes you will see a picker-up with five or six dogs. The picker-up's job is to stand in the background with his dogs at heel while all the shooting is going on and to mark and remember the falls. At the signal that the drive is over, the picker-up starts sending his dogs to retrieve the downed birds. He will send each dog individually for the birds he's marked, sending for the runners first.

During the Victorian era, shooting was exclusive to the land-owning gentry. The changes wrought by decades of major economic adjustments and two world wars have changed that. Today, the typical shoot is a syndicate (group) composed of successful businessmen who rent the sporting rights of a piece of land and manage the shoot themselves. The size may range from shoot days of two hundred to four hundred birds down to the do-it-yourself syndicate who shoot over a local farm, do all their own gamekeeping, and consider it a great day if they get fifty birds.

Shooting is a significant industry in the United Kingdom today. Shooting pumps £2 billion ($3.32 billion) into the United Kingdom economy annually. Shooting in the United Kingdom supports the equivalent of seventy-four thousand full-time jobs. There are thirty-five hundred full-time gamekeepers. One-third of the United Kingdom landmass is managed for shooting. This management necessitates a proliferation of small woods, small cover, hedges, and managed boundary coverts. These features are beneficial for all wildlife.

In England, the gundog is essential to the shooting industry. He is critical for the dogging-in when the young pheasants are newly released. He is necessary for the orderly flushing. He is necessary for collecting all the downed birds at the end of a drive. He is essential for collecting the inevitable runners. With the revenue produced by pheasant at £25 to £35 ($41 to $58) per bird and by grouse at £80 ($133) per bird, shoot owners don't tolerate dogs that are poor at finding birds. Similarly, they don't tolerate dogs that are noisy or out of control, as this disrupts the shooting and costs them revenue and customer goodwill.

Here are some representative costs in 2014:

Shoot	Birds	Guns	Price per gun
Blenheim Palace	300 - Pheasant & Partridge	8	1,850 GBP ($3,000)
Arley & Eymore	150 – pheasant & Partridge	10	500 GBP ($830)
Ripley Castle	250 – pheasant & Partridge	9	915 GBP ($1,500)

Source: www.gunsonpegs.com

During the Victorian era, as the sport of shooting evolved during the second half of the eighteen hundreds, the role of the gundog was defined by the same man that planned and developed the working model of driven shooting. That man was the gamekeeper. The gamekeeper designed and planted the crops and trees for the driven shooting. He procured, raised, released, and cared for the "crop" of pheasants. The gamekeeper defined the role of the gundogs and the behavioral standards for the shooting. He generally also bred and trained the gundogs. From that gamekeeper culture and custodianship arose the gundog with the behavioral traits vital to game-bird shooting. Those important gundog traits are game-finding initiative and a propensity for cooperative self-control. These are the important traits in a gundog wherever and whatever you are shooting, be it grouse in Scotland, partridge in Spain, or ducks in the United States.

UNITED KINGDOM RETRIEVER FIELD TRIALS

The other major feature figuring into the history of the gundog is the field trial. The first retriever field trial in the United Kingdom was held in 1899. The retriever field trials, then and now, continue to reflect the influence of the gamekeeper culture on the traits to be desired in a gundog. The realities of shooting requirements continue to drive breeding selection, as field trials can only be conducted on actual shoots. The field trials must keep the gamekeepers and shoot owners happy in order to be invited back. Therefore, noisy, unruly dogs and handlers are not tolerated in field trials.

Here is the introduction of the (British) Kennel Club rules for retriever field trials:

Introduction
   a. Field Trials *shall be conducted in accordance with the Kennel Club* Rules and Regulations.
   b. A Field Trial is a meeting for the purpose of holding competitions to assess the work of Gundogs in the field, with dogs working on live unhandled game and where game may be shot.
   c. Game that has been handled in any way, either dead or alive, must not be used for testing dogs in any part of a Field Trial, except that dead game may be used in the conduct of a water test.

Field trials have great significance in the driving of breeding selection in gundogs. The breeder and the marketplace are both
basically driven by the numbers of field trials titled parents on a
dog's pedigree. The more Field Trial Champion titles there are on
a dog's pedigree, the more likely the dog will be bred. The more
Field Trial Champion titles there are on a puppy's pedigree, the
more people will desire to buy him. A very pertinent question in
this equation is, "What are the underlying dog behaviors valued by
the judging culture that awards the field trial placements that produce the Field Trial Champion titles?" Those underlying behaviors are what are being selected for. In the United Kingdom, those
behaviors have historically been, and remain today, game-finding
initiative and self-control in a high-distraction environment.

Countess Lorna Howe was an early participant in British field
trials beginning just after World War I. She judged, made up many
field champions, and was a prominent figure in the field trial world
for many years. With respect to field trials, she wrote in the fifties:

> It should always be remembered that trials were original-
> ly started to find out the best dogs for recovering game
> that is shot and to breed from these dogs to carry on such
> strains....It was always impressed on one that retrievers
> were not sheep dogs, that their first and most important
> work was to find game—particularly wounded game.

These words are as true today as they were in the early nineteen
hundreds.

Here is a vastly simplified synopsis of the rules for retriever
field trials in the United Kingdom today:

- Twelve dogs for one-day trial; twenty-four dogs for two-day
  trial
- No more than two dogs for one handler

- No delineation of amateur or professional
- If the dog has poor line manners, he is out.
- If the dog makes any noise, he is out.
- If the handler is noisy, he is out.
- If the dog creeps, he is out.
- Cripples are retrieved first.
- If the dog fails to find the bird, he is out.
- The next dog is sent for it.
- If the dog chases freshly flushed birds, he is out.
- If the dog is tracking a cripple and flushes a fresh bird and chases it, he is out.

In the United Kingdom, the retriever field trial is still doing a good job of driving breeding selection to produce good gundogs, dogs that are high in the behavioral traits of game-finding initiative and cooperative self-control. United Kingdom field trial judges place a very high value on good manners in the face of high distraction, as in a dog sitting calmly in a group of dogs for twenty or thirty minutes while scores of pheasants are driven over and shot.

Great value is also placed on tracking a cripple and retrieving it. It is normal procedure for a dog to be asked to pick a particular cripple in spite of other dead birds lying about. If, while tracking the cripple, the dog flushes fresh birds and chases them, then the dog is dropped from the trial. The next dog in line will then be asked to find the crippled bird.

Many judges want to see both behaviors from a dog before awarding him a place in a field trial. Occasionally, you will see a trial in which no places are given, because the judges didn't see performances worthy of awarding points toward a field trial title. Obviously, the judges take quite seriously their stewardship of the breeding-selection function of field trials. They understand that the purpose of field trials is to enable better breeding selection for superior gundogs.

Another facet of great significance was built into the United Kingdom field trial rules. A limit is placed upon the number of competing dogs: Twelve dogs for a one-day trial and twenty-four dogs for a two-day trial. A further limit in United Kingdom field trial rules is that no more than two dogs may be handled by one handler.

The significance of these limits is very visible in breeding selection. Ninety percent of field trial champion titles are won by dogs that are owned, trained, and handled by an amateur. That means 90 percent of those titles were won by dogs that were trained by a novice trainer as opposed to a professional trainer. Thus, those 90 percent were probably high in trainability and were probably fairly easy to train. In the US field trial system, those statistics are reversed. Probably 90 percent of the field trial titles are won by dogs that are owned by amateurs but are trained by a professional trainer.

In the United Kingdom, the first retriever field trial was in 1899. These field trials have continued forward in their original intent as a driver of breeding selection to produce better gundogs. The retrievers are an integral part of a very large shooting industry. The fact that field trials are dependent on landowners and gamekeepers to be invited to conduct the trial on a shoot gives the gamekeepers and landowners a strong voice in keeping the field trial desired behaviors relevant and valuable to the shooting.

The queen has also been a very strong influence in keeping retriever field trials relevant and valuable to the shooting industry. For many years, she has maintained a kennel of Labradors and Sandringham. When the royal family shoots at Sandringham, the queen takes some of her Labradors and picks up. Additionally, she holds a field trial annually at Sandringham in which she either judges or competes with one of her dogs. She also hosts, every three to four years, the International Gundog League Retriever Championship at Sandringham or Windsor.

In short, the queen is an enthusiastic supporter of retriever gundogs and a knowledgeable and skilled owner and handler of retrievers. I would surmise that when she sees judging practices starting to trend away from real-world shooting needs, she whispers in an ear or two and influences a course correction.

FIELD TRIALS IN AMERICA

In America, the first retriever field trial was held in 1931 and run with British rules. We in the United States started with the British field trial model because we imported it from England along with the gamekeepers, dogs, and pheasants. In the twenties and thirties, a small group of very successful businessmen in the northeastern United States became enamored of Victorian shooting parties and proceeded to import them. They built large estates and brought in pheasants, gamekeepers/dog trainers, and gundogs, and started hosting shooting parties styled on the British model.

They subsequently held the first retriever field trial in 1931 at Robert Goulet's Glenmere estate at Chester, New York. This retriever trial was run under the British model, and the British model continued for American field trials through most of the 1930s. The significant turn from the path of producing good gundogs came in 1936. Some of Averell Harriman's friends were tired of being beat in field trials by the Harriman dogs running under Harriman's imported Scottish gamekeeper/trainer, Tom Briggs.

In 1936, the friends set up a field trial and created the amateur stake, restricting the participating dog handlers to amateurs. Within a few years, the amateur stake was written into AKC rules. The rest of the change was the exclusion of professional trainers from judging field trials and serving on AKC advisory committees. Thus was the corporate body of dog knowledge and the gamekeeper culture removed from the field trial system.

The amateur architects of the new retriever field trial system built a system that no longer fulfills its original purpose of enabling and promoting the purpose of driving breeding selection of better gundogs.

The major flaw was the failure to provide a mechanism to deal with increasing numbers of dogs entering field trials. As this phenomenon arose in the late forties, the amateurs doing the judging started resorting to contrived, artificial methods to separate dogs. These artificial methods were based on the basic principle that Mother Nature designed dogs to take the energy-efficient route from point A to point B. They began to set up tests that had energy-expensive obstacles between point A and point B. Dogs that deviated from the line between point A and point B by taking the energy-efficient route were penalized.

US retriever field trials were born of a contest between gamekeepers/dog trainers and amateur dog handlers. The amateur dog handlers removed the dog trainers from the field trial system through changing the field trial rules, and those amateurs built a system that drives breeding selection to produce better field trial dogs, but that fails in breeding selection to provide better gundogs. The breeding selection that results from such a field trial judging process produces a high percentage of dogs that are too tightly wound for ease of training and too highly driven for the average hunter to enjoy hunting with.

The US retriever field trial system has failed at its original and primary purpose, which was to produce better gundogs.

CHAPTER 18

An Elephant in the Room

———

I GET A LOT OF phone calls from hunters seeking gundogs. Most of the phone calls begin with the statement, "I am looking for a hunting dog, not a field trial dog." That is a good sign. The American hunter is becoming much more aware that good field trial dogs frequently make poor hunting dogs. The population of field trial dogs contains far too many dogs that are high in reactivity and low in impulse control. This makes a dog that is difficult to train and difficult for the average guy to keep under control. They are a lot of work. I am going to give you a tale of just two dogs who have contributed their genetic traits, both good and bad, to the gene pool of field trial retrievers. Many other dogs with similar traits continue to contribute to that gene pool as well.

This is a tale of two retriever gundog faults that have become widespread. The faults are whining in the duck blind and inability to sit still in the duck blind. The spread of these faults is a signal that our retriever competitions are failing at their job of guiding breeding selection to produce excellent gundogs.

I have been conducting an informal survey for the past few years. At every retriever seminar I conduct and whenever I am thrown together with waterfowlers, I ask, "How many of you are duck hunters?" Then I ask, "How many of you have been in a duck blind with a whining dog?" The resulting response is nearly 100 percent of duck hunters have been in a blind with a whining dog.

That is absolutely astounding. Thirty years ago, you never saw a Labrador that was an excitement whiner. Today, obviously, there are many excitement whiners in the duckdog ranks. Genetics is involved with excitement whining. A lot of today's whiners probably have in their pedigrees a particular sire that was a National Amateur Field Trial winner in the early seventies. This dog had been fairly noisy on shot flyers in his youth, and some fairly strenuous training was required to suppress it. It was suppressed sufficiently to only occur a little bit every once in a while in a field trial. The dog only occasionally voiced a small whine, which field trial judges forgave because the dog had so much style as expressed by his moving fast and flashily on a retrieve. This dog won a Canadian National and a US National Amateur. He was a very popular dog and was bred to many, many bitches. You can suppress an individual dog's behavior, but that does not suppress the inheritance of the trait by his puppies. This dog produced a lot of noisy offspring that eventually led to the prevalence of the trait today. Unfortunately, the concept of a little bit of whining is about as valid as the concept of a little bit of pregnancy.

Another common retriever gundog fault today is an inability to sit still in a high-temptation environment. When guns start shooting and birds start falling, this dog starts bouncing and can't sit still. In field trial dogs this is typically manifested as creeping. When the shooting starts the dog moves forward unbidden and gets well out in front of his handler. Creeping is very undesirable in a gundog. One of the best creepers that I have ever seen won a National Amateur Field Trial in the early seventies.

The professional trainers customarily serve as bird throwers at the National Amateur. The year in question, I was throwing birds and thus watched every dog run. The dog in question I will call "Creeper" to protect the guilty. Creeper was a quite talented dog. Every time a bird was thrown, he would creep out ten feet from the handler. When the bird reached the top of its arc, Creeper would turn unbidden and zip back to heel, while marking the bird's fall over his shoulder. If it was a triple, where three birds are thrown sequentially at three different locations, Creeper would upon each throw, zip out ten feet in front of his handler and return unbidden like a yo-yo, winding up each time back at the heel position.

Creeper won the National Amateur that year. He crept on every thrown bird. Obviously, the judges gave little heed to the creeping. They probably forgave the creeping because the dog had so much style. He charged out with great effort, speed, and accuracy, and excelled at the tests that the judges had set up. They forgave the creeping for the sake of "style."

However, by condoning the creeping, they did a disservice to the gundog world. When a dog gets to the national level of competition, you can bet that money, effort, and training have not been spared in trying to smooth out any behavioral issues. If the creeping could have been suppressed by training, it would have been. Thus, one can assume that there was a significant genetic component to Creeper's creeping. Being a National Amateur Field Champion, Creeper was bred a lot. He produced a lot of puppies. A significant percentage of those puppies had a strong tendency to creep.

Both whining and creeping are symptoms of an underlying behavioral makeup. They are both symptoms of a dog who is high in reactivity and low in impulse control. Such dog does well at field trial work, where excellence is based upon the principle of the dog taking the energy-expensive route on a retrieve. Such a dog is also likely to be difficult to train.

The hunter needs a dog that is low in reactivity and high in impulse control. That dog will be easy to train, easy to live with, and pleasant to have in the duck blind.

Over the last thirty years, the dog that is high in reactivity and low in impulse control has spread prolifically in the field Labrador gene pool. To gain a perspective on how fast a genetic behavioral trait can spread, one only need look at the Silver Fox Tameness Research Project conducted in the sixties by the Russian geneticist Dmitry K. Belyaev.

In Russia, there are a number of farms raising wild foxes in large pens for the fur industry. Belyaev went to a silver-fox-raising farm and conducted a breeding-selection research project. He went through the farm and selected a number of foxes. His selection was based upon each fox's tolerance of people. He selected foxes that tolerated a close approach by a human. He then bred these "close-approach" foxes with each other. These pairings produced first-generation offspring that tolerated being touched by humans. The breeding according to greater affinity for people continued. By the fifth generation, the pups were friendly toward experimenters, wagging their tails and whining.

In the sixth generation bred for tameness, they produced some fox pups that were eager to establish human contact. The fox puppies whimpered to attract attention and sniffed and licked the experimenters, just like dog puppies. The experimenters termed this behavior category as "domesticated elite." By the tenth generation, 20 percent of the experimenters' breeding population was domesticated elite.

The silver fox experiment is a great example of how fast breeding selection can change major behavioral traits. It took only ten years to go from a population consisting of 100 percent extremely wild foxes to a population of foxes that were mostly tame, with 20 percent of the population extremely tame.

Looking at the field trial gene pool of Labradors, one can say that in the fifties and sixties, most of the field trial dogs were fairly calm. They were low in reactivity and high in impulse control. Then, as the amateurs judging field trials began to change their standards and began to allow creepers and whiners to win field trial titles, the gene pool began changing. More titles went to dogs high in reactivity and low in impulse control. Those titles also went on pedigrees, and people used those pedigrees to select breeding candidates. We have been pursuing this course for forty or fifty years now. What percent of Labradors in the field trial gene pool now are high in reactivity and low in impulse control? It is probably very high.

When there is an underlying important and obvious topic that everyone is aware of, but which is not discussed because such discussion is uncomfortable, the phenomenon is sometimes referred to as "an elephant in the room."

With respect to the US field trial Labrador gene pool, there is an elephant in the room. The elephant's name is "style" or "drive" or "straight line." When you next want to select a gundog puppy, you would be well served to look behind the elephant. Look past the pedigrees and personally meet the puppy's parents. If the parents don't behave the way you would want, then the puppy is unlikely to behave the way you will want.

CHAPTER 19

Teaching Tales

EAT RIGHT (OR LEFT) TO LEARN BLIND RETRIEVES

THE OLD MAN WALKED SLOWLY along the riverbank with the boy and a young Lab puppy. The boy had just arrived home for a three-month vacation. The puppy, six-month-old Sadie, had been with the old man since she was eight weeks old. The old man occasionally puffed a pipe as he ambled along, enjoying the sunset and the company of boy and puppy. Sadie divided her attention between the old man, the boy, and a myriad of new scents to explore. She came up to each person periodically for a brief pet and greeting before moving on to the next sight or scent of interest.

Ocasionally, the old man gave a soft tweet on a whistle, at the sound of which Sadie would spin, sit, and look at him. Immediately, when she sat, the old man gave her a, "Good dog," as he briskly stepped over to her and gave her a treat.

"She surely sits crisply," stated the boy. "Why are you blowing the whistle so softly?" he questioned.

"Her hearing is four times as sensitive as yours is," replied the old man. "She can hear at 100 yards a sound that you can barely hear at 25 yards. If I train her to respond to a loud whistle right next to me, then she is not going to respond well to the soft sound she hears at 150 yards."

As they walked along, the old man next dropped a dummy on the path and heeled Sadie along away from it. When they were thirty yards distant, he turned and sat Sadie. He sent her back toward the dummy, stopping her with a soft whistle tweet at ten yards.

At the tweet, Sadie turned and sat looking at the old man. He tossed a dummy off to the right and waited a couple of seconds before casting her to it. Upon Sadie's return, he sent her back down the path for the thirty-yard dropped dummy. Sadie took off for it with alacrity. When she reached fifteen yards, the old man gave a whistle tweet that cued her to stop and look at him, which she did.

The old man exclaimed, "Good dog," and let her sit a couple of seconds before giving her a back cast to go onward and collect the dummy.

The old man stopped walking and relit his pipe, taking a puff or two. The boy recognized the signs and got ready to listen to the coming lecture. "Sadie learned all this stopping on the whistle and casting by my feeding her properly," said the old man. He continued:

"Starting with her first meal, I would hold the bowl up until she sat. Sitting caused the bowl to come down on the ground for her to eat. Then I progressed to sitting her, moving away a couple of steps, and lowering the food bowl. When Sadie got up, the food bowl went higher. When Sadie sat down, the food bowl went down closer to the ground. Over the course of several meals, I was ten feet away, and Sadie learned that sitting calmly got the food bowl down onto the ground. Then we progressed to her sitting a second or two after the bowl was down and then sitting twenty or thirty seconds after the bowl was down, and she was released with a hand signal toward the bowl."

The old man walked over to a stump, sat down, and resumed his narrative:

"The next was to get a whistle stop while Sadie was going somewhere. I used raising the food bowl as the cue for sitting. I first stopped her when she was coming toward me and could see the cue.

"She had already learned that the bowl moving up meant 'Sit' and that sitting produced the reward of the bowl coming down to be eaten. To begin, I sat Sadie and walked off twenty feet with a food bowl. I turned, waited a bit, and called her to come while lowering the bowl a little. When she had come ten feet toward me, I gave a tweet on the whistle while raising the bowl. She stopped and sat. I waited a second or two and gave her a click or a 'Good dog' while putting the bowl on the ground. She arrived and ate."

The old man paused and relit his pipe, taking a puff or two before continuing:

"After three sessions, she was 90 percent reliable on sitting to the tweet, so I upped the ante a little. I sat Sadie, walked thirty feet from her, and put down the food bowl while watching her to make sure she stayed. Then I walked four steps back toward her and positioned myself about three steps off her approach line to the waiting bowl. I gave her a hand signal toward the bowl, releasing her with 'Over.' When she was halfway to the bowl, I gave her a tweet accompanied by a step toward her approach path to the bowl. She stopped and sat. I clicked or said, 'Good dog,' waited a couple of seconds, and cast her onward to the bowl. We now had a behavior chain of: go—stop and sit on whistle –- cast onward---, reward. When Sadie was quite proficient on stopping and casting to and from food bowls, and also quite steady on thrown dummies, we swapped the behavior to dummies."

The boy sat with Sadie and listened patiently to the old man's lecture. The boy said, "Thank you for getting Sadie from Dr. Stanton's last litter. She is a really nice dog, and she is certainly well trained."

The old man replied, "Sadie's training was easy and fun. When training is mainly delivering rewards, it is great fun for Sadie and me both. She is fairly well started in the behaviors needed for blind retrieves, but she needs lots of practice performing those behaviors in the face of increasing distraction. She needs to perform easy, blind retrieves when guns are shooting, in moderate cover, in water, in new locations—all the factors that increase the difficulty for a dog to perform."

"What about marked retrieves?" asked the boy. "My buddies mostly go out and work their retrievers on marked retrieves."

The old man cocked his head to the side and smiled. This was a topic he warmed up to. He said:

"Boy, retrievers are born with the talent of marked retrieves. If an ancestral wild dog was unable to watch a bird land off in a field, go over, hunt him up, and eat him, then that ancestor died. Performing marked retrieves is something retrievers are born with. It does not need training. To the contrary, marked retrieves are such a strong, instinctive behavior that they make it harder for a dog to learn blind retrieves."

He lit his pipe and took a puff or two, and then, pointing the stem at the boy for emphasis, continued:

"Blind retrieves are not natural to a dog, and they require a good bit of training. The objective is to build up the value of a blind retrieve so that it can compete with the strong, innate drive of marked retrieves. We build that value with many repetitions of the behavior chain: Go, —stop on whistle –– cast onward––– reward. Every time we pay that sequence with the reward at the end, we are building the value of blind-retrieve behavior. After a large number of payments, the behavior becomes valuable enough to compete with marked retrieves. That's when you start doing a few marked retrieves. Remember, a retriever's primary function is conservation. His most valuable behavior is to leave the dead, marked retrieves lying and go get the long unseen cripple that will be lost if not retrieved quickly."

Retriever Gundogs
and Field Trials

————

IT WAS A COLD, WINDY October Saturday. Rain steadily pattered against the windows. Dove season was over. Nearly two months spanned the long wait for duck season. The wind was too high to fish. The boy was a pain in the neck. The old man thought that the time was propitious for a lesson on dogs.

"Boy," growled the old man, "come in here next to the fire, and we are going to have a little lesson on duckdogs. Sit in that chair there and listen while I tell you about codfish and Labradors and fowling pieces and gundogs."

"Yes, sir," said the boy somewhat reluctantly.

"Boy," said the old man, "I am going to broaden your knowledge with a little history. The Labrador retriever is the best duckdog in the world today, and he got his start catching codfish for British fishing fleets. In the fifteen hundreds and sixteen hundreds, they used to fish in the summers off the coast of Newfoundland. They caught the cod on long hand lines back then and didn't have barbed hooks. A lot of fish flopped off of the hook on the way into the fishing dory, and a dog that could catch the momentarily dis-oriented fish more than earned his keep."

The old man paused to light his pipe and continued, "The next big step for Labradors came in the eighteen hundreds. The inven-tion of breech-loading shotguns gave birth to a great appetite for shooting birds in England and Scotland. King Edward VII was an avid shooter and drove the development of a whole culture of driven shooting. Grouse were a favorite, and pheasants were a prime target. Great stature and importance was attached to production of large numbers of birds by gamekeepers. The great estates were judged by the numbers of birds shot and collected. It didn't take long for folks to figure out that a good retriever found more birds in tough cover and tracked down enough cripples to get the numbers up. They also found that calm, well-behaved dogs did not frighten birds and thus helped the numbers. The Labrador found his niche in life."

The old man paused and stepped over to stir up the fire. He gazed out the window for a moment. Then he continued, "The British were pretty smart. When they figured out how great was the benefit of a good gundog, they put a quality-control process in place. They started field trials to identify the dogs that were really good at their job, so that they could breed better and better dogs. They were smart enough to hold the trials in the working field, and they evaluated the dogs while they were performing the actual job. They knew that anytime you let people start interpreting the dog's job, the people would screw it up. The British field trial system has been in place since 1900 and is today still producing great gundogs that are calm enough to sit for driven birds and expert at tracking down crippled birds."

The old man got up and began pacing, heralding a major pronouncement. With a negative head tilt, he announced, "In America, we have gone down a different path with retrieving gundogs. In the United States, in the twenties, rich northeastern seaboard sportsmen started copying the British Edwardian shooting party. They bought big estates, built big houses, imported British and Scottish gamekeepers, and duplicated British driven shooting. They also imported Labrador retrievers. The first American retriever trial was held in 1931 in New York, and it was run under British rules. For about ten years they stayed with the British field trial model, which served well for breeding selection to produce better gundogs."

He stopped and took his glasses off, pointing them at the boy. The boy braced himself, for this meant a major declaration was coming. "Then the northeastern sports rewrote the rule book. They divided field trial folks into professionals and amateurs and barred the professionals from judging and from serving on advisory committees to the American Kennel Club. This effectively separated the professional trainers from the business of designing field trials. The end result was supposed to be judges that designed tests that tested the qualities of a good gundog."

The old man replaced his glasses and pointed a finger at the boy. "What they got was a bunch of judges that made up tests evaluating whether or not a dog was an energy conservationist. Mother Nature designed the dog's ancestors to be conservers of energy. The less energy the ancestor used, the less game he needed to catch to survive. As soon as these eastern sport judges figured that out, they started to set tests that allowed them to eliminate the energy conservers. They would set up a test where it was hard work to follow the straight line to the bird. Then they penalized the dogs that followed their natural tendency to take the less-work route. They might put a bird on the far side of a pond. The dog that simply ran around the pond was penalized. The dog that took the hard-work route, swimming through the middle of the pond, won. Now, that is a way of separating dogs in a field trial, but it is not a satisfactory evaluation of a dog's game-finding talent. Finding birds is the only valid test of game-finding talent."

The boy spoke up, "Well, Billy's dad has a great field trial dog, and he says that it is important that they go in a straight line."

The old man's eyes glinted, and the boy knew immediately that he had walked into a trap.

The old man responded, "Billy's dad has it half right. Field trial dogs are one thing; gundogs are another. It is important for the field trial dogs to go in straight lines. It is important for gundogs to get the birds quickly and efficiently. It is important for field trial dogs to be under precise control and be handled to the exact spot where the bird is. It is important for gundogs to hunt up the dead birds and track down the cripples whose locations are fuzzy and often guessed at."

Looking out the window and then back at the boy, the old man said, "The bottom line is a man has to decide whether he wants a field trial dog or a gundog. For a field trial dog, the behaviors judged are not natural and require a lot of training and mainte-nance training. For a gundog, the behaviors are generally natural and easy to train. They don't need a lot of maintenance training. The gundog behaviors are easily judged by counting how many birds are collected."

The old man glanced again toward the window, and he said, "It looks like it is clearing a little outside, so we need to wind this up. I want you to train my new Lab puppy, and I want her trained as a gundog, so you only need to train two behaviors. The most im-portant is steadiness. She needs to sit quietly in a high-distraction environment, such as one hundred ducks circling while several gunners are shooting. In temptation level, that is very similar to a British driven shoot."

He picked up his pipe and pointed, saying, "Then she needs some directional control. When the shooting is done, and there are four dead ducks floating out in front of the blind, while a long un-seen cripple has sailed one hundred yards out to the right, the dog needs to get the long unseen cripple first, before he has a chance to swim off. This requires whistle-stopping and hand signals."

The old man gave a slight grin and said, "Now, the weather looks broken sufficiently for you to hike down to the pond and catch me a couple of fish for dinner. Take your fishing dog with you."